Praise for L

"Thank you, Linda Carroll, for this clear ad
challenging, stages of love. It's so good to   e
are also pivots of growth, and above all th   t
become even more deeply connected in th

— Daphne Rose Kingma, author of *Coming Apart* and
The Ten Things to Do When Your Life Falls Apart

"Linda Carroll has achieved it — a truly commonsense manual on growing relationships while growing ourselves. *Love Cycles* is a must-read for all, no matter where you are in your cycle of loving. Kudos to Carroll for a valuable contribution to a discipline long in need of a 'real' model."

— Marilyn Mason, author of *Facing Shame: Families in Recovery*

"If you want a road map to love, if you want to love more deeply, if you desire a way out of pain — this book can serve as a kind companion."

— Pat Love, EdD, author of *Hot Monogamy* and
How to Improve Your Marriage without Talking about It

"Linda Carroll is a seasoned couples therapist who has written a very engaging book that urges individuals and couples to understand and adopt her approach to genuine intimacy. Her chapters on Wholehearted Loving are worth the price of the whole book."

— Barry McCarthy, PhD, author of *Rekindling Desire*
and *Sexual Awareness*

"This beautifully written book is replete with valuable information about the cycles of love. The author has enlivened the narrative with concrete examples of couples in each stage and empowered couples on the journey from the romantic tingle to wholehearted love with effective, time-tested exercises to build the skills to get there. We recommend it to all couples."

— Harville Hendrix, PhD, and Helen LaKelly Hunt, PhD,
authors of *Making Marriage Simple*

"Wise and immediately helpful, *Love Cycles* speaks to every couple — brand-new partners in the throes of infatuation, seasoned couples struggling with doubt and discontent, those who have been shattered by an affair or other betrayal, and those who confront the crossroads of intimate partnership: Do we split, or do we recommit? Linda Carroll deeply understands the challenges and potential of each stage and will help you normalize, survive, and master this journey."

— Janis Abrahms Spring, PhD, author of *After the Affair:
Healing the Pain and Rebuilding Trust When a Partner Has Been Unfaithful* and
How Can I Forgive You?

LOVE CYCLES

LOVE CYCLES

The Five Essential Stages
of Lasting Love

LINDA CARROLL

foreword by SAM KEEN
quiz by PEPPER SCHWARTZ
and LINDA CARROLL

New World Library
Novato, California

New World Library
14 Pamaron Way
Novato, California 94949

The material in this book is intended for education. It is not meant to take
the place of diagnosis and treatment by a qualified medical practitioner or
therapist. No expressed or implied guarantee of the effects of the use of the
recommendations can be given or liability taken.

Text design by Tona Pearce Myers

Library of Congress Cataloging-in-Publication Data
Carroll, Linda.
Love cycles : The five essential stages of lasting love / Linda Carroll ;
foreword by Sam Keen.
     pages   cm
Includes bibliographical references and index.
ISBN 978-1-60868-300-0 (paperback) — ISBN 978-1-60868-301-7 (ebook)
1. Love. 2. Intimacy (Psychology) 3. Self-actualization (Psychology) I. Title.
BF575.L8.C24437 2014
152.4'1—dc23   2014014810

First printing, September 2014
ISBN 978-1-60868-300-0
Printed in the USA on 100% postconsumer-waste recycled paper

New World Library is proud to be a Gold Certified
Environmentally Responsible Publisher. Publisher certification
awarded by Green Press Initiative. www.greenpressinitiative.org

10   9   8   7   6   5   4   3   2   1

For Tim

Linda Caul

As a whirlwind
swoops on an oak
Love shakes my heart.

— SAPPHO, as translated by Mary Barnard

I am so grateful to you, my many clients and students who for the past thirty-five years have shown up for therapy and the Love Cycles program with openhearted trust and bravery. To protect client confidentiality, all details and identifying information in cases and anecdotes have been changed, mixed, and in some cases reinvented.

CONTENTS

FOREWORD

Love is a many-splendored thing: The essence of God. That old black magic.

Intimate warfare. The end of hostility. A game of hide-and-seek. Chemistry (caution: sometimes what you thought was H_2O turns out to be H_2SO_4). The answer. Please repeat the question! Sweet madness. The only sanity. The cure for loneliness. The élan vital that binds all things together.

It is appetite, fancy, favor, liking, craving, yearning, enthusiasm, esteem, appreciation, distress, disappointment, anger, respect, adoration, fidelity, ardor, caring, lusting, worshiping, cherishing. And much more.

I have spent a good deal of my life in the pursuit of love in its many forms — eros, agape, philia, and libido. I like to believe

I have made some modest progress in becoming someone who loves well, if only because I now understand my past failures.

I wish I had come upon *Love Cycles* a few decades ago. It would have repurposed my romantic illusions about falling into effortless love and helped me to understand that creating enduring love is always a work in progress, requiring mastery of many skills and an abundance of self-knowledge forged in forgiveness, acceptance, and celebration.

Linda Carroll has created an elegant, smart, and practical love map, rooted in modern science and ancient wisdom, for a lifelong journey. By identifying and describing the five stages of love, she helps us to avoid getting lost in the labyrinth and going around and around in a vicious circle.

This rare and exceptional book offers us both a useful map of the geography of love and an introduction to the skills necessary to become someone who loves well and is well loved.

— Sam Keen,
philosopher and author of many books, including
Fire in the Belly and *To Love and Be Loved*

INTRODUCTION

When you love someone, you do not love them all the time, in exactly
the same way, from moment to moment....We insist on permanency, on
duration, on continuity; when the only continuity possible, in life as in
love, is in growth, in fluidity — in freedom, in the sense that the dancers
are free, barely touching as they pass, but partners in the same pattern.

— ANNE MORROW LINDBERGH, *Gift from the Sea*

This book provides a road map to the myste-
rious, difficult, and wondrous journey of wholehearted love. It
offers a framework for following love's path, combining insight
into the latest research on the physiology and psychology of love
with practical techniques for managing conflicts and developing greater intimacy. *Love Cycles* presents a model that is easy to
grasp, drawn from my counseling work with couples and individuals since 1980 and the many teachers and modalities of training
I have been fortunate enough to have worked with. I also draw
from my lifelong study and love of the wisdom found in ancient
mythology, poetry, songs, folklore, and spiritual traditions.

I hope this book will offer you a deeper understanding of a
relationship's inevitable conflicts, a reflective space in which to

examine your own choices, and a guide to strengthening your connection with your partner. Finally, I hope that this book will serve as a reminder that intimate relationships are, most of all, an "inside job."

One of the grounding principles of *Love Cycles* is that love is not merely an emotion but a practice, a daily ritual we undertake. To love truly, deeply, and well is to accept that love is hard work and requires commitment to every step of the journey. Practicing love involves a set of skills — skills we will explore in depth in these pages. It also involves a commitment to play, to enjoy, and to spend time together in connection. Finally, the stages of love do not end at wholehearted loving but rather with an acceptance that the stages form a spiral; different ages and stages continue to bring new gifts and fresh challenges. Over time, we become more flexible and willing to accept the natural impermanence of relationship seasons.

To begin this journey, we must work against two ingrained ideas about committed relationships—convictions that are passed along by our culture's narratives about love. The first idea is that "love is all you need." If we look long and hard, this narrative tells us, we will find that one "right" person who can connect deeply with us, end our loneliness, and meet our every need. Once we find this soul mate, we will be forever enmeshed in the bubble of a shared psychic home, our anxieties and isolation melting away under love's perpetual glow. The second, opposing idea is that long-term love is an impossible dream. When we look at the appalling divorce statistics, remember our parents' and/or friends' disastrous marriages, and reflect on some of the disappointing relationships in our own pasts, we may want to run away from love shrieking. This instinct to protect ourselves often leads to serial monogamy, uncommitted hookups, and sworn singlehood.

Yet despite our doubts and fears, we return again and again to the riches that love offers. We've all heard stories about people on their deathbeds who dismissed as trifling the money, power, and other worldly treasures they'd amassed, acknowledging that all that had truly mattered was how well they had loved. In our own lives, most of us have experienced the joy that comes from weathering stormy times in an important relationship and coming through it with a capacity to love that is stronger than ever. We want to love as powerfully and fully as possible. This quest — what I call the five stages of love — is a vital human adventure whose promise calls to each of us.

Love Cycles devotes a chapter to each of these five stages. Some of us may cycle through the stages many times with one person over the course of a long life. Others of us may change partners along the way, either integrating what we've learned into each new relationship or repeating painful patterns until we learn how to create the relationship we want. The stages remain the same, whether we've been with the same partner for decades or have recently become impassioned at our fiftieth high school reunion. Certainly, with increasing wisdom and self-awareness, we may move through the stages more gracefully and swiftly over time. However, I don't know of any straight, simple path that takes us directly from falling in love to wholehearted loving.

The first stage, which I call the Merge, is the beginning romance of love, in which we experience our partner as a thoroughly delightful — even perfect — soul mate.

Next is stage two, Doubt and Denial, which we experience once the love drug wears off and we settle into more predictable routines with our partner. In this second stage, we begin to see our lover in a new, less flattering light. This chapter looks at how we wrestle with this stage's central conflict — between who we want our partner to be and who he or she actually is. In a follow-up chapter, called "Six Essential Skills," we explore to how to keep our relationship on track in the face of inevitable disappointments and differences.

When couples have trouble dealing with differences effectively, they arrive at the third stage, Disillusionment. At this point, the conflicts of the second stage have grown and become magnified, and many partners enter an all-out power struggle characterized by self-protective strategies, grudge bearing, and sometimes outright betrayal. This chapter highlights the stories of several couples in my therapy practice who have teetered on the brink of serious, relationship-threatening conflict.

In stage four, Decision, the couple has arrived at a crisis, which I call the "wall." At this point partners are forced to make a decision about the future of their relationship. In this chapter I lay out the possibilities and limitations of four key choices: leaving the marriage, staying together but miserable, leading parallel lives, or working to transform the relationship.

Stage five, Wholehearted Loving, describes a stage of love that not all couples arrive at together. It comes about when we choose to work hard on the relationship and embrace both the difficulty and the possibility of this transformational path. In this chapter I also address how those who do not make it as couples can still become whole and happy on their own.

We do not always move progressively through these stages in one steady line. Love's journey takes a form more like a spiral, in which we can find ourselves back in earlier stages even after a long relationship. You will find a quiz right after chapter 12 to help you identify the stage you are currently in. Learning the dangers and wisdom of each stage gives us insight into the path ahead, allowing us to take the long view of our relationship, even when we feel mired in disappointment or conflict. It reminds us that these stages are inevitable rather than a sign that we are with the wrong person. It reminds us that although learning to live with, and love, another person is difficult, this challenge can spur wisdom, growth, self-knowledge, and abiding connection.

Love Cycles is the book that would have aided me in various stages of my own journey. It is the information I wish I had when I was eleven years old, feeling the first surge of hormones at the sight of a particular boy. Having no basis for understanding healthy attachment, my feelings for him became an obsession that lasted for years; I was convinced that the pounding in my heart and my inability to think of anything else meant we were destined for each other. I held onto the fantasy that he was the "one" until I met him again as a full-fledged adult and realized that though he was still enormously appealing, he and I would have made a perfectly disastrous couple.

Love Cycles is the book I wish I had in my twenties, when I fell into a series of relationships with men who were altogether wrong for me. Mistaking a shared need for connection, protection, and intimacy for the presence of a soul mate, I found myself in inappropriate relationship after inappropriate relationship — each of which ended in acrimony and sadness. It is the book I wish I had at forty when, after years of soul-searching and learning to be happy with my own company, my heart and head told me I had found the right person. But we had few skills to deal with the endless conflicts that emerged between two strong-willed, opinionated people. My husband and I, now married for twenty-five years, were committed enough to find teachers and practices that set us on the path described in this book.

Over the years, as I've listened to individuals and couples in therapy describe their intimate relationships, I began to notice a distinct pattern. While each relationship had its own distinct dynamics and challenges, all of them seemed to follow the stages that I describe in this book. I share some of their stories here.

But the book also springs from my own circuitous path toward creating a healthy partnership. As someone who has struggled mightily with every aspect of intimacy and who has firsthand experience of love's intensity, danger, and promise, I offer my hard-earned wisdom and the humility that accompanies it. After hearing my story, someone once said to me about creating a thriving relationship: "If you can do it, anyone can!" It is this fundamental optimism about love's renewing power that animates *Love Cycles*.

Chapter One

THE MERGE

An oceanic feeling, when everything comes together,
oneself, everyone else, the world, and divinity,
it is like the feeling that you get when you stare out
at the infinite reach of the ocean: it is a little frightening,
but it is also awe-inspiring and exhilarating.

— WILLIAM JAMES, *The Varieties of Religious Experience*

To fall in love feels more miraculous than anything I know. Life is infused with magic and fresh meaning. During this first giddy stage of intimacy, new lovers merge, much like a mother and her newborn child. Boundaries melt away, and the sense of "we-ness" is all there is.[1] Our similarities seem profound, our conversations endless. If anything threatens to point out our differences, we rush to rationalize it, convinced that our beloved's qualities and quirks are just the "right" differences. *Okay, so he barely talked to my friends tonight, but that's because he listens so well! I plan everything, but she's so spontaneous — just what I need to get out of my rigid rut.*

Our similarities excite us, no matter how obscure. We both loved the same song in the seventh grade. We both have always wanted a golden Pekingese, and we both harbor a secret desire to climb Machu Picchu. It all becomes evidence that we are about as perfect as two human beings can be for each other.

In many ways, the advent of love is a transcendent experience. There is sacredness in this first stage; it is not simply an illusion. We are truly able to sense the other's spirit. Just as important, we experience our own brightest light. One of the most marvelous aspects of this stage is not only the idealized way we see our partner but the new, more laudable way we see ourselves. Listening closely comes easily to us, as does giving the ideal response. Our patience seems eternal, our interest in the other boundless. Who knew that we possessed such generosity, such largeness of spirit? How delightful it feels to live with an open heart, bountiful compassion, and unconditional care.

In the shelter of our love bubble, it's easy to think we can float in such pure happiness forever. Yet no matter how strong the bond may become later, the exhilaration of early love isn't sustainable. Somehow, each of us must find our way back to ourselves.

Charlie and Megan: An Oceanic Start

They make a striking pair. Megan, a high-level health-care administrator with a sharp-edged, regal beauty, is the sort of woman people might describe as an "ice princess." Charlie, a pediatrician, is the kind of big, shambling man whose gentle friendliness puts people instantly at ease. It's no surprise that children love him.

Megan remembers the first time Charlie walked into her office to introduce himself as a new member of the hospital staff. He was undeniably good-looking and clearly accomplished. He had graduated from medical school with honors and spent the next two years in Sudan, where he cared for orphans. He had every reason to take himself seriously, even to be a touch self-satisfied. Megan knew plenty of doctors like that.

Megan could see, though, that this man was different. As they chatted, it became clear that Charlie had a heart as well as a brain. Later, she was even more impressed when he introduced an animal-assisted therapy program at the hospital so that seriously ill children could cuddle and play with dogs especially trained for the program and even visit with their own beloved pets.

Charlie also had a well-developed inner clown. Megan registered this fact as soon as she caught sight of his tie, which peeked between the lapels of his white lab coat. It was the first of many "magic" ties she would see, whose cavorting animal patterns were guaranteed to distract and delight sick children. "I wish every pediatrician had your sense of play and fun," she told him.

In the weeks that followed, Megan found herself increasingly drawn to Charlie. The effect his presence had on the children in the wards touched and amazed her. As for his effect on her, he enlivened their every encounter with zany humor. His personal warmth was unfamiliar to Megan, whose family was undemonstrative. Something in her stirred. With him, she began to feel nurtured, not unlike the children under his care.

So when Charlie asked her to join him for coffee one afternoon, she readily accepted. Lunches in the hospital cafeteria followed, which led to weekend concerts and, soon, to amorous evenings at his apartment or her condo.

The delight of the unexpected left Megan giddy. She had broken through the barriers of her careful, upper-class Philadelphia upbringing to join a stranger in a strange land. She loved to listen to Charlie tell stories about life in Oregon on the farm, where he'd grown up as the son of a taciturn rye grass farmer. Hunting and harvesting were as novel to her as the bear hugs Charlie gave her in the hospital corridors. When they made love, Megan felt herself unfold. She had been taught to weigh every decision, but now there was no decision to make. She simply surrendered.

And Charlie? At first he was tempted to dismiss Megan as too highbrow, a woman whose sophistication overshadowed his simple, homespun tastes. At the hospital he often heard her tell her colleagues about the latest art exhibit she had seen. At the staff Christmas party, she said how exciting it was that "finally, we'll hear *Aida* this month," as though everyone else on the pediatric ward had season tickets to the opera. There was, however, something vital and alive about her that intrigued him. Beneath her reserved surface, he sensed a playful personality just waiting to emerge.

By the time Charlie met Megan, his life had changed so dramatically that he barely recognized it. He had achieved many of his dreams — to become a doctor, to travel the world, and to enhance the lives of small children through medicine and laughter. He had gained enough confidence to flirt with a woman who might well have intimidated him in the past. In fact, Megan's initial coolness only heightened his interest. When she responded, he was ecstatic. Her blue-green eyes seemed to see right into his soul.

Surrendering to Romance

When we fall in love, our rational minds may try to raise red flags to warn us that, once we step across love's threshold, there will be minefields and sinkholes. Megan, for example, dimly realized that Charlie's fun-loving nature sometimes embarrassed her. Occasionally, Charlie felt rebuffed by Megan's reserve.

Most of us know all about red flags. Experience may well have taught us that the initial passion won't last and that pain and loss will inevitably follow. But we fear the risk of greater loss if we turn away. Anyway, that's not usually an option! In the first stage of love, our emotional brain pummels our rational brain into submission. Caution and fear fall away, and we submit to the pleasure and power of romance.[2]

Human beings possess two distinct and opposing instincts: the desire to merge with another and the need to remain an individual. Both are vital. Just as an infant and mother bond, so do newly joined lovers become immersed in each other. And just as the infant must one day push against her mother to become herself, we, too, need to eventually move away from our lover and recover the edges of our own uniqueness. For the moment, however, to push away is the last thing we want to do. We want to merge — and why wouldn't we?

Some lovers try to stay inside the love bubble as long as they can by creating their own private culture. They invent a language of their own that nobody else can understand. They share jokes with punch lines that are funny only to them. Within the perceived safety of the bubble, their merge feels at once total and eternal. It was in just such a bubble that film star Ingrid Bergman and her husband, Petter Lindstrom, named their daughter, Pia, with the three letters standing for Petter, Ingrid, Always.[3] Alas, the marriage fell apart, but Pia's name remained a reminder of love's possibilities and its fragility — always.

Of course, not everyone experiences the "urge to merge." Some people never feel it at all. Or they enjoy an initial hit of ecstasy that quickly dissipates. Some people enter love slowly, with a friendship that gradually leads to an intimate partnership — one that may or may not be spiced with romance. Others choose a partner because they feel that "it's just time," which may coincide with the accelerating ticking of the biological clock. Still others focus on similarities based on ethnicity, race, religion, education, class, and life goals. Indeed, in many cultures, selecting a mate has little or nothing to do with falling in love. Nonetheless, so much of our culture — songs, movies, fairy tales, and novels — leads us to believe that idealized love is the norm. We await the prince who will kiss us awake or for the princess who will melt our heart and soul.

A Kind of Madness

This first stage of love has been chronicled for as long as human beings have been on the planet. Often lovesickness is cited, brought on by the intense changes associated with falling in love. Ibn Sina, tenth-century physician and father of modern medicine, viewed obsession as the principal cause of lovesickness.[4]

We now know that he was right. The biochemical changes that take place in new lovers produce symptoms similar to those in people with obsessive-compulsive disorder, including loss of appetite and sleeplessness. Charlie, for example, lost ten pounds during the first three months of knowing Megan; he found that he simply wasn't hungry. Megan, meanwhile, slept fitfully, just four or five hours a night.

How well we know the signs of obsession: fantasies of the beloved fill our days and crowd our nights. When we're apart, we feel incomplete. If absence makes the heart grow fonder, it also leads to constant chatter about the missing object of affection. This fixation and preoccupation are what others find tiresome about the love-struck. People roll their eyes and think us temporarily insane. Which, of course, we are.

In 1979 psychologist Dorothy Tennov coined the term *limerence* to describe this temporary state of madness and described the conditions associated with it:

- overestimation of the good qualities of the beloved and minimization of the negative

- acute longing for the object of one's affection
- feelings of ecstasy in the presence of the loved one
- deep mood swings from ecstasy to agony and back again
- involuntary, obsessive thinking about the other
- deep agony when the relationship ends[5]

The list reminds me of Stu, an old client of mine (and a recovering alcoholic). Stu told me about the first time he got drunk at age fourteen: "We had beer and wine hidden in the trunk and pulled the car over to try it. My friends took their time, but the moment I took my first drink I was hooked, and I bolted down the second one almost before I had finished the first. I passed out that night and got really sick. My friends were also ill and didn't go near alcohol for months. Me, though? I couldn't wait to have another drink. Wine was all I thought of. The sun rose and set on that longing. I craved the next drink the way my friends longed for a girlfriend."

It startled me to hear how his words could just as easily have described what it feels like to fall in love. "I just had to have it" and "I just had to have her" do not seem very far apart.

New lovers do have much in common with addicts. Magnetic resonance imaging reveals that the nucleus accumbens, the part of the brain that is activated in lovers, is the same part that lights up in cocaine users and gamblers when they act out their addiction.[6]

This recent discovery brings to mind the old adage: magic is science not yet understood. What we do know, however, is that the craving associated with romantic love is very real. Greek mythology provides us with imaginative and amusing ways to describe the felt intensity of romantic love. Aphrodite, the goddess of love and beauty, had a son named Cupid. His job, as an archer, was to dip arrows into his mother's secret love potion before he took aim. Once Cupid's arrow hit its target, the victim fell madly in love with the next person he or she saw. This myth has given rise to some of the most extraordinary love legends of all time, including those of Apollo and Daphne, Helen of Troy, Antony and Cleopatra, and Romeo and Juliet. We now know that the "hit" of romance can be partially explained by biochemistry. Science tells us that the pounding heart that leaves us breathless, trembling, and longing to be with our beloved signifies an overabundance of particular chemicals and hormones in the brain and blood, including PEA (phenylethylamine), a natural amphetamine also found in chocolate and marijuana.[7]

As they float on a sea of PEA, lovers report more sensational and adventurous sexual experiences than they've ever enjoyed before, such as "mile-high sex" (sex in an airplane bathroom) and a heightened pleasure in sensory qualities that might normally be a turnoff. Napoleon Bonaparte, for example, once wrote to Josephine, "I'm coming home. Please don't wash."

As if a generous shot of PEA weren't enough, the love cocktail is also spiked with endorphins, which boost pleasure and decrease pain, and oxytocin, a hormone that promotes bonding and cuddling. This cocktail infuses us with euphoria and extraordinary energy, which is why sleep and nourishment seem unimportant. Our perspective becomes so skewed that we see only what is good and beautiful in our lover; we're blind to all else.

Science notwithstanding, I think a poet can describe the situation best. Perhaps no one has captured this first stage of love as well as the English poet John Keats in his letters to his wife, Fanny Brawne. Here is an excerpt from one of them: "I cannot exist without you. I am forgetful of everything but seeing you again. My Life seems to stop there; I see no further. You have absorb'd me. I have a sensation at the present moment as though I was dissolving....Love is my religion. I could die for that; I could die for you. My Creed is Love and you are its only tenet. You have ravish'd me away by a Power I cannot resist."[8]

A Suitable Mate

To fall in love is natural. For love to last is not. Long-lasting love results from the necessary work that two people do — the self-work, primarily — to create a strong, durable partnership over time. Each partner must participate in this strenuous effort. We're more likely to succeed if we've chosen our partner wisely in the first place.

Alas, there's the rub. The strength of our romantic feelings does not signify that our beloved is a good partner for us. In fact, we may suffer from "love jerk syndrome," the tendency to fall madly in love with someone who is continually hurtful or who lacks emotional maturity or self-control. Or we may fall for a Narcissus, who sees only his or her reflection and cannot create a relationship that makes room for two.

Some of us may seek the excitement of unrequited love. Nothing tantalizes like intermittent reinforcement, or hot-and-cold love. A kind and faithful partner may not attract us; we fear that he or she would bore us. For some, the idea of "taming the shrew" or "loving a bad boy into a good one" is irresistible — and usually disastrous.

To choose well is harder than it looks. We are biochemically and psychologically primed to select a certain type of mate. Our DNA compels us to find and mate with someone to produce the healthiest offspring possible. Therefore, we seek diversity — someone who is different from us. At this level, whether or not our partner is a brute is beside the point; it's the genetic blend that matters.[9] Research by Harville Hendrix and Helen Hunt, cocreators of Imago Relationship Therapy, has led them to conclude that the chemical cocktail that accompanies the Merge is "nature's anesthesia, which numbs us to the knowledge that we are falling in love with an incompatible person." According to Hendrix and Hunt, every person carries an Imago, or an inner image of the combined traits of our primary caregivers — some of their best traits and definitely some of their worst. Our attraction to a particular partner is an opportunity to finish the business of childhood, to put us back in touch with our original wounds so that we can finally heal them.[10] Our mother may have been unduly critical or our father overly authoritative, and guess what kind of person we will look for in a partner?

Recall Megan, who disarms Charlie with her blue-green eyes. Her hidden penchant for criticism and her need to take charge will be far more fateful for him than her soulful gaze. Yet such an attraction has a deeply hopeful element. In his choice of Megan, Charlie has found a person to help him resolve emotional problems that linger from childhood, which can be accomplished only with a partner who demonstrates the very qualities that most challenge him. In her choice of Charlie, Megan is faced with sorting out her mixed reaction to his childlike silliness and over-the-top humor, the very qualities she was raised to deny in herself.

Two things are going on here. For psychological reasons, we gravitate toward a person who can help us heal old wounds. For biological reasons, however, we're not fully in charge of what attracts us. If we have such limited control over our selection process, is there really any such thing as choosing a partner wisely? Yes — up to a point.

We can choose to pay attention to our loved one's history, integrity, and level of self-awareness. How does he speak of past lovers and partners? Is she able to acknowledge her part in situations that haven't gone well, or is it always someone else's fault? What kind of relationships does he have with his family members? (No trouble and all trouble are both "trouble.") One of the most important ingredients in a happy, long-term relationship is a person's ability to take responsibility for conflict and learn to apologize and make amends. How a person has handled these things in the past gives us important information about how she's apt to handle them in the future.

In other words, although we can't override our chemical or physical attraction to another person, we can choose not to move toward what may not be good for us. Perhaps more important, we can avoid any permanent decisions while we're in this stage. Get to know your partner before you marry, have a baby, move to Cleveland together, or take any other step with major consequences. Find out who she is when she's angry or disappointed. At the same time, do your best to commit to a rich, fully dimensional life of your own — even if such a notion seems ridiculously irrelevant at the moment. You won't be sorry.

The Path to Love

Learning to love well is the crowning achievement of life. Love helps us to heal from trauma and to bear unimaginable burdens. It helps us to live longer and happier lives. As neurobiological research has recently taught us, love alters the pathways of the brain, strengthens the immune system, and contributes to healthy heart and organ functions.[11] Universally, love is the key to our continuation as a species. Individually, love unlocks our greatest potential.

Again, as most of us know, the path to such heights isn't an easy one. Creating a thriving relationship that can withstand change, loss, and the passage of time is one of life's most challenging endeavors. When we fall in love, we may believe we've been saved from vulnerability, disappointment, and loneliness. Rather, we've accepted an invitation to know all three in a new way — through the kind of growth in our character and spirit that we couldn't have imagined possible.

Once we emerge from the Merge, some of us will be able to reunite with our lover with new maturity and deeper, if perhaps less intense, satisfaction. It depends on our ability to reconcile two distinct needs: to dwell in the delights of the other and to stand firm in our own space. Some of us learn this delicate balancing act more easily than others, but there's no hurry. Each of us moves at our own pace as we travel through the next three stages — Doubt and Denial, Disillusionment, and Decision— before we reach the fifth and final stage, Wholehearted Loving. Journeying through love's five seasons will help us to accept that love will never stop changing, to accept the rain, thunder, and sunshine that are all part of love's nature. To be truly wholehearted allows us to accept the wholeness and to accept with equanimity the message of Buddhist teacher Pema Chödrön, who wrote in her deeply insightful book *When Things Fall Apart*, "We think that the point is to pass the test or to overcome the problem, but the truth is that things don't really get solved. They come together and they fall apart. Then they come together again and fall apart again. It's just like that. The healing comes from letting there be room for all of this to happen: room for grief, for relief, for misery, for joy."[12]

The most crucial outcome of all is our commitment to grow through relationship, which will allow us to reclaim the best in ourselves and become happier, more fulfilled individuals.

Chapter Two

DOUBT AND DENIAL

O lovers! Be careful in those dangerous first days!
Once you've brought breakfast in bed you'll have to bring it forever,
unless you want to be accused of lovelessness and betrayal.

— MILAN KUNDERA, *The Book of Laughter and Forgetting*

It has to happen. Sooner or later we begin to chafe in our cocoon. The merge with our lover feels less than ideal — indeed, not quite natural. We begin to miss our ordinary lives, old friends, and former pleasures. We want to do things with other people or simply be by ourselves.

Meanwhile, certain things about our lovers, which used to be so charming, begin to grate. Her gregariousness now seems a touch insincere, his reliability rather rigid.

What if this person isn't really as magnificent as we thought he was? What if we're not meant for each other? But how can this be?

No sooner do we feel the first twinges of doubt than we begin to push them away and deny their existence. Indeed, we often experience this second stage of love as a series of dance steps. First, our partner says or does something that makes us spring away in alarm. As our doubt and fear arise, however, we stomp on these feelings, and then we try to tap-dance our way back to "the way things were."

Many of us do this tap dance exceedingly well: we reinterpret our first fight as a testament to a love that can meet any challenge. We characterize our partner's defensiveness as "oversensitivity" or our own oppositional responses as "strength." At least for a little while we manage to reassure ourselves that everything will remain blissful. That's why this second stage tends to be the silent stage, the one we don't discuss. We smooth over anything negative, too fearful to broach it with our partner, lest we make things worse and destroy what we still think of as our perfect happiness.

There is no escaping reality, however. Slowly but surely, the love drug that makes us feel so smitten begins to dissipate. Sooner or later, the love bubble pops, and we can no longer deny it: differences between us do exist — and they do cause us problems. To our profound disappointment, we must admit that our love isn't perfect. Human beings are annoying, and our beloved is no exception. Rapture wanes, and we find ourselves with a partner who can irritate, disappoint, and step on our toes. We begin to criticize, and we're dismayed to find that our lover finds fault with some of our behavior, too.

This transition is painful, but it's not a catastrophe. In fact, our emotional and relational health depend on it. For each of us to move forward in our development, we must face the fact that we're different people with distinctive needs that will never mesh entirely.

In the initial merge of love, our partner's differences were good qualities to embrace. We were willing to shuck some of our own tastes and habits because our partner seemed destined to make our life bigger, brighter, and better. She, the computer engineer, left behind her programming job to go backpacking in Alaska with her beloved mountaineer. The solitary ornithologist, meanwhile, set aside his binoculars and let his new Argentine lover teach him how to dance the tango.

We know we've traveled beyond the first stage when we shake our heads in amazement at the enthusiasm we mustered in order to plunge into something that goes so against our grain. How could a computer geek ever have agreed to weeks in the Alaskan wilderness, given that she found the outdoors more irritating than inspirational? The bugs drove her crazy, and the long treks through the woods were exercises in boredom. Meanwhile, the ornithologist now squirms when he thinks about his dismal attempts to learn the tango. He felt like a fool out there on the dance floor, and he must've looked like one, too. Whatever had caused him to humiliate himself so thoroughly?

Another way to tell we've shifted from the first stage to the second is our altered physical state. Now our body language cries "beware" rather than "welcome." In place of the love cocktail, new and less pleasant chemical processes kick in to complement our doubt and denial. Stress hormones set off some primal responses — we want to fight, flee, or freeze.

The boundless lover in us is benched, and we send in our street fighter, our ice queen, or our frightened deer. The tactics we choose to protect ourselves are often the ones most feared by our partner. We fall prey to "infinity loops," the bane of every relationship.[1] They work like this: I, who fear rejection, discover that you fear intimacy. As you push me away, your aloofness makes me feel abandoned. Panicked, I attempt to draw you closer, which in turn makes you retreat even more. And around and around we go.

Oh, No — We're Different!

In the second stage, the "Why aren't you me?" question arises. Why don't you see the world as I see it? Why don't you place the same value as I do on sharing, saving, and spending? Why don't you want the same kind of social life that I do? Why don't you see books, pets, movies, and sports with the same eyes that I do? Such questions are very common, and we'll explore them in greater depth in a later chapter.

To make matters worse, we may discover that we have contrasting libidos. Because the chemical cocktail experienced in the first stage is an aphrodisiac, people with naturally low libidos experience a temporary elevation in their desire level. Sex, after all, is a quite literal way to merge. But as romantic feelings abate, some people find it difficult to feel turned on, while partners with higher libidos may feel increasingly frustrated and rejected.[2]

Because few of us are aware that these shifts in attitude and behavior are normal, we begin to think that something is wrong with us. As a couple, we buy into one of the most popular misconceptions about love: if the relationship is right, sex will happen naturally and be of equal pleasure to both partners. *This is not true.* A person with high testosterone will think of sex more often and may be attracted to other people. A person with a lower "t-count" will think of sex less frequently and may find it difficult even to feel aroused. Unfortunately, many people with low-libido partners conclude that they are no longer attractive or loved.[3]

As these sexual differences emerge, they add to our sense of threat. We see them as another sign of our fundamental incompatibility. Our worry may grow into real fear that our love affair is headed toward the abyss.

Doubt's Echo Chamber

In our anxiety, we tend to compare our eroding relationship with those of the couples around us, all of whom appear blissful. Media hype about the soul mates of the month (It's Angelina and Brad! No, wait, now it's Justin and Jessica!) contribute to our worry. Perhaps if we'd chosen a better partner, the enchantment wouldn't be fading and we, too, could claim the perfect relationship, just like the one between Prince William and Kate Middleton.

Laced with imagery about undying passion, our culture teaches us that if we have conflicted feelings and thoughts about our partner, it must mean the relationship is wrong — or is already over. In fact, ambivalence is a normal human feeling. Single people sometimes long to be in a relationship, and people in committed relationships sometimes wish they were single. You can love and hate the same person at different times of day — or even at the same time. You can also love your partner and still fantasize about your first love.

To harbor such thoughts and feelings doesn't mean that your relationship has gone bad. It simply means you're human. It's what we do — or don't do — next that separates us from the crocodile and the red squirrel, one of the most libidinous creatures on the planet.

To think sometimes about your college girlfriend isn't a problem. To resume contact with her, however, means you've likely crossed the line.

Learning to Steer

Although nothing promises to bring us more joy than love, becoming a couple also makes us vulnerable to receiving our deepest wounds and to behaving as our most frightened, reactive selves.

What we often fail to realize is that this second stage leads us to a crucial gateway. Our passage through it permits us to move closer to the possibility of real, abiding love. As romance recedes, we don't have to fight, flee, or freeze. We can learn to steer through difficulty in ways that deepen our capacity for resilience and support the relationship rather than threaten or damage it.

When two people share a life, they naturally have two points of view on how to live it. They may differ on matters of life and death and everything in between — the type of car to drive, where to vacation, which political candidate to vote for, which charity to fund — not to mention how to celebrate the holidays with family. They might even have quite different perspectives on matters of health and personal hygiene. Most of us don't know how to manage differences or collaborate in the midst of conflict. We tend to polarize, merge, or just give up. The strategies we use arise from our family history, personal experiences, genetic makeup, and the unique ways our personality manifests itself.

Avoiders evade a problem or try to please their way out of it. Withdrawers stonewall, disassociate, or disappear. Fighters press to win. Although each of these approaches is a normal, instinctual response to conflict, none is conducive to collaboration. These responses create fallout that we eventually sweep under the carpet. After a while, the rug gets mighty lumpy, and we start to trip on it with increasing frequency. As we stumble, we tend to believe that our partner is responsible for the lump. What we rarely notice is our own contribution to all the bulges.

Megan and Charlie: A Good Myth

Several months into their relationship, Megan felt bold enough to introduce Charlie to her family. The occasion was the seventieth birthday of her ultraconservative father, to be celebrated at a dinner party at one of the New York's most formal and celebrated restaurants. As always, Megan packed carefully for the trip and chose her clothes for the event with utmost care. Formality was called for here, not imagination. Charlie, already in the city for a conference, had left a few days earlier and was planning to meet her at the hotel. Megan put on a little black dress and a string of pearls and waited for him in the lobby.

As the time for his arrival neared, an alarming thought flitted across her mind. What if he showed up in one of his magic ties? It wouldn't be the first time he'd worn one of these novelties outside the children's hospital; in fact, he sometimes wore them at seminars, like the one he was now attending. In the past she'd been embarrassed but said nothing. After all, they'd only been out at the movies, at casual gatherings, or in a meeting room with other pediatricians. Tonight's occasion, of course, was anything but casual. Surely Charlie would remember that. She had explained to him that they were expected to dress up, that her parents were very traditional people.

When Charlie arrived, Megan's heart sank. Although he was well dressed in every other way, his tie featured Koko the Gorilla. Battery-operated lighting effects made the animal look as if he was turning cartwheels. Megan knew her parents wouldn't appreciate this brand of humor, not at a formal event. Hadn't Charlie considered this? Why would he wear this stupid tie if he cared about her, as he claimed he did?

Strongly tempted to tell him to take off the tie, Megan somehow held her tongue. The cab ride to the restaurant was silent as she turned things over in her mind. Maybe Charlie needed to take a stand? The tie was a way to shout, "I am not an East Coast sophisticate." She sensed, too, that he wore the tie to test her: "Do you love me as I am?" And by extension, to test the two of them as a couple: "Aren't we as one?"

Well, sure. She would never forget that first thrill of liberation when she had decided that Charlie was the one for her. She had taken a leap, and he had caught her. He helped her move beyond a rule-obsessed family culture that she found suffocating. They were in this thing together.

At the restaurant, everyone was polite enough, but nobody welcomed Koko. Her mother pursed her lips as the gorilla turned a somersault. Her father rolled his eyes. "Very clever," he said, as Koko winked, but he didn't really think so; that was clear.

For the first time, Megan saw Charlie through the critical eyes of her parents and old family friends. The shift in perception was disturbing. Although she tried hard to shake the impression, she felt less and less attracted to Charlie as the evening wore on. In conversation with her mother, a political science professor, Charlie couldn't hide his limited knowledge of, or interest in, current events.

"There's a new resident from Czechoslovakia on the ward," he said. "He's got a lot of interesting information about the differences in the hospitals here and there. I think we could learn a lot from how they deal with children as patients."

"Oh?" Megan's mother perked up and seemed genuinely interested. "I suppose your resident is too young to have grown up with the Communists. I have a good friend at the university who was still there when the Soviet troops moved in. Grim days indeed. He's Slovakian. I suppose your colleague is Czech?"

"Well, he's from Czechoslovakia, so, yes, he must be Czech." Charlie laughed nervously.

"Not necessarily," she corrected him. "The Slovaks didn't split off into their own country until the early nineties. They remain a small minority in the Czech Republic even today."

"Ah, yes. The Czech Republic," Charlie repeated. "Right, well, I'm not great with history. But I've always liked the name of that revolution, the sound of it. It reminds me of the Velvet Underground, one of my favorite bands, not that I still listen to rock music these days." There was that nervous laugh again.

Megan's mother nodded and began to scan the room. "Excuse me," she said to Charlie. "I see someone else I need to greet."

Megan's heart sank as she watched her mother lose interest in her "perfect prince," a man who knew so little about European history. As Megan's mother walked away, Charlie looked relieved.

Later, when he joked with her father and his friends, the love of Megan's life no longer sounded witty and original. He sounded naive and childish, even goofy. She prayed he wouldn't bring up his recent hunting trip out to Oregon.

To reassure herself, Megan later cornered her mother to brag about the stack of impressive awards that Charlie had received for his medical work. "You know, Mom, Charlie has won one of the most prestigious awards in pediatric medicine two years in a row," she said. "I think he gave up sleep for an entire year!"

Then she crossed the room to tell her dad about the almost magical effect that this gifted doctor had on upset children and his gentle way of handling the most difficult patients in the hospital. Relieved by her own praise, she settled back into the calming conviction that the man she loved truly was remarkable.

The weekend following the party was spent in polite (and careful) visits with family friends. Megan behaved as though everything was going wonderfully.

Still, she had been shaken. There had been a moment at the birthday party when the lights went on in her head and she saw that Charlie wasn't the monument to perfection she had erected in her mind. She'd banished the dreadful insight as quickly as it came. Eager to move forward with their plans to marry and start a family, she couldn't afford to think "bad thoughts" about Charlie.

Like most of us, Megan reacted to early warning signs of difference by denying them. In her case, she laid her discomfort on her mother. "I couldn't believe her face when she saw your tie," she said to Charlie later. "What a laugh that was!"

For his part, Charlie rationalized Megan's aloofness toward him at the party as the kind of straitlaced behavior seriously conservative people expected from their daughter. Each of their interpretations was meant to prove how strong their union was.

The marvelous myth of perfect union isn't easy to give up. We'd have so much to lose, or so it would seem, were our love bubble to pop. So we fight off our doubt to hold on to bliss. Thus Megan and Charlie took preventive action. Neither of them wanted to feel that sense of alienation ever again. When they returned to Oregon, without a word Charlie donated all his silly ties to a charitable group that put on parties for sick children. Without a word, Megan began to buy more acceptable ties for Charlie — soft-colored silks, hand-folded ones, even a bolo. Soon Charlie needed an extra rack in his closet to hold them all.

At first Charlie was touched by the discreet way that Megan had chosen to signal her desire that he dress stylishly and appropriately for every occasion. Slowly, however, he began to notice the many other ways she tried to redirect and manage him. Her gift subscription to the *New Yorker* arrived with a jesting comment: "Just wanted to make sure you know lots of clever things besides those cute kid jokes." As she watched him read the gift card, Megan's mouth curved into a smile. Her perfect, white teeth were dazzling against her olive skin.

Charlie was reminded of how much he admired her. The care she took with her appearance: her thick, shining hair, perfectly manicured nails, and chic business attire. He loved her for her subtle yet sharp way with words. She went to the heart of the matter with no need to raise her voice. Never mind that she sometimes used her verbal skills against him. That she often bested him wasn't something he was ready to admit to himself.

Clearly, Megan and Charlie were in the denial phase of this second stage. "Stuffing" their differences would see them through for a while. Once we notice our differences, however, we only tend to notice them more, no matter how hard we try not to. Our contrasts become larger, clearer, and more upsetting. If a couple stays stuck in denial, they will likely become more and more alienated from each other. The good news is that this doesn't have to happen. There is a way forward.

Chapter Three

SIX ESSENTIAL SKILLS

How it is that animals understand things I do not know,
but it is certain that they do understand. Perhaps there is a language
which is not made of words and everything in the world understands it.

— FRANCES HODGSON BURNETT, *A Little Princess*

We need skills for many of the important things we do in our lives: driving, practicing our profession, and even teaching our dog to heel. Why do many of us expect that the feelings of the Merge will carry us into loving relationships? We know from research that although most couples have many of the same troubles, the one difference between those who thrive and those who dive are the skills they develop. Over the years I've noticed six skills that prove necessary to the well-being of any committed relationship:

1. understanding your part in the trouble
2. listening without barriers
3. accepting your differences and learning how to collaborate

4. making a new move
5. nourishing the relationship (especially when you don't feel like it)
6. keeping your own tank filled

Not surprisingly, these skills tend to build on one another and sometimes to converge. If you're able to keep an open mind, you're more likely to develop the six skills and integrate them all into one masterful resource.

Skill 1. Understanding Your Part in the Trouble

It's difficult to have real exchanges with our partner if we're not clear about our needs and motivations. First we must be honest and listen to ourselves. Then we must be honest and listen to our partner, in good faith. Otherwise, so-called communication is nothing more than an empty exercise. Here's an example of this dynamic, which played out in two meetings with a couple I saw in my practice.

As Rob and his girlfriend, Mandy, sat in my office, Rob spoke enthusiastically about his weekend. He'd just come back from a "fantastic celebration," his twenty-fifth high school reunion, but he hadn't invited Mandy to go with him.

"I feel excluded," Mandy said, looking down at her feet. "I know you wanted to spend time with old friends, and I actually thought that was great. Except you didn't ask me to come." She hesitated for a moment. "I felt like maybe you weren't proud enough of me to introduce me to your friends."

"I'm really glad you shared," Rob said, leaning in close to her. "I can understand how you feel." He capped his response with a smile and a hug.

Mandy settled back in her chair, somewhat mollified.

The following month, Rob took the lead in planning a

weekend ski trip with some of the same friends. Once again, he failed to invite Mandy. This time, when he began to "actively listen" to her feelings of exclusion, she jumped up and strode out of my office. Rob sat there, amazed at his girlfriend's negative reaction. He worked in an industry whose products were cutting-edge, and glitches in the newest systems often led to consumer complaints. He was a master at grievance management. The communication skills that worked so well in that environment were ones he used in one-time interactions with customers. With Mandy, however, he ran into trouble. She had begun to witness enough repeat performances of his listening to her protests with all the right responses, while continuing the same old behavior, to see them for what they were — well-practiced management techniques rather than genuine listening. Although Rob was in couples counseling, he seemed unwilling to learn how to listen to his partner with the necessary empathy, curiosity, and willingness to change that allow real growth in a relationship.

If Rob had used his considerable communication skills to connect rather than to manipulate, he would have heard Mandy's pain about not being invited to the school reunion rather than just pretending he had. Out of respect for her feelings, he might have then asked her along on the ski trip or come clean and explained his needs for time alone with his old friends.

Your Emotional Core

If you get stuck in behavior that doesn't work, as Rob did, it's time to explore your emotional core. Reflecting on your family history and understanding its impact on you is one of the best ways to get information about how you operate in your intimate relationship. My experience as a therapist has taught me to look out for two red flags when people recall their childhoods. The first flag pops up when I hear that "everything was perfect," and the second when I'm told that "everything was awful."

The story of a perfect childhood is one of omission. No one escapes entirely from the human condition and its trouble, loss, fear, and difficult passages. We might prefer memories in which everyone smiles in the photograph, and the message says "Happy Holidays from the (Perfect) Family." But our real history is more complicated. Every family is made up of moments and seasons, and every sibling is born into a different family, in terms of how she reacts to circumstances and how she interacts with other members.

If you remember your childhood as perfect, your rosy remembrance is probably a reflection of your positive personality and perhaps your adherence to a family value that admits only to the flawless. If you believe that everything in your childhood was bad, that belief, too, reflects your personality and your family ethos and is most likely an overstatement. If things were so uniformly wretched, where did you get the skill and the courage to read a book like this? To go to work, make dinner, find friends, and maintain hope that life will get better? (Of course, some people have enjoyed reasonably happy, safe, and loving childhoods, while others have grown up with a lot of struggle, pain, and fear. It is the 100 percent stories — all bad or all good — that I am addressing here.)

Not all the clues about how we interact and behave can be found by looking at our families, of course. Some people who come from solid, caring homes find themselves at a perpetual loss in adulthood. Others who grew up in poster families for dysfunction manage to build rich, happy lives. Nonetheless, every family wields a lasting impact. All of us can benefit by revisiting our beginnings and paying special attention to the childhood beliefs and behaviors that we bring into our present relationships.

In Good Faith

In fairness to Rob, effectively engaging in a conversation that involves a complaint is one of the trickiest skills to master in relationships. Often our partner's grievance with us has more to do with him and less to do with us than he thinks. If we don't listen and hear him out, however, he'll never see his part in the problem.

When, on the other hand, the problem has more to do with us and we refuse to recognize that fact or make amends, we hurt our partner, the relationship, and ourselves. We need to own our part in the trouble we're facing. And usually, we do play a part. None of us has met our spiritual and psychological potential. None of us has flawless emotional intelligence, and none of us ever completely overcomes a judgmental mind or a tricky heart.

Nonetheless, we can learn how to better detect when and how we cause trouble, do the necessary repair, and then move quickly from our inevitable struggles to a genuine reconnection.

Be aware, though, that effective communication doesn't simply result from new, more articulate ways to express criticism, give advice, and press our point. The underlying reason for most communication problems is that we're trying to get our partner to see our truth, to understand our feelings, or to do it our way rather than looking for a bridge between us.[1]

For communication to be effective, it must allow for a different outcome than the one we think "should" happen. Otherwise, our conversations deteriorate into empty exercises like Rob's exchanges with Mandy or into a war of words as we return to the old question, "Why don't you see things the same way I see them?"

As most of us have experienced firsthand, impulsively speaking our minds isn't always the wisest move, either. We need to exercise self-restraint to avoid damage and destruction, especially when we're angry. We need to employ certain auxiliary skills, too, so that when we do disagree, we're able to resolve our differences in ways that support our needs as individuals and as a couple.

When my friends Jodi and Alden were out for a walk one morning, they entered a leash-free zone where they let their shepherd, Sparky, roam. A feisty dachshund was on the scene, and suddenly the two dogs got into a fight. Sparky bit the dachshund's neck. The bite was serious enough that the owner had to take his pet to a veterinarian for stitches.

Legally, Jodi and Alden weren't responsible for the vet bill because the fight took place in a leash-free zone. Ethically, however, Jodi felt obliged to pay it.

Alden was against the idea entirely. In fact, the other dog owner had angered him. It was reckless to let an animal as uncontrolled as that dachshund run free. Also, Jodi's high ethical standards got on his nerves sometimes, and they did so now. He took a few moments to control himself, however, before he said anything. He reminded himself how Jodi's standards often worked to his benefit and that they were admirable, even if he didn't share them. By the time he finally spoke, his anger had died down, and his voice was calm and even toned.

"I don't think that's necessary, Jodi. The law is on our side, and that dachshund was looking for a fight. He was nipping at Sparky and circling him from the moment we entered the park."

"Yes, but Sparky is so much bigger."

"If we pay, we'll just encourage that guy to let his dog run wild. Next time he might get really hurt or hurt another animal."

"I see your point, Alden. Well, let's think about it," Jodi said quietly. If it were up to her alone, there'd be nothing to think about; she'd just pay the owner and be done with it.

Each felt in the right. However, neither pressed the point.

They listened to each other and then gave themselves some time to decide what to do. Although Alden didn't want to pay anything, he accepted his partner's strong opinion about a moral obligation. Although Jodi wanted to pay the bill in full, she likewise accepted the fact that Alden had a point of view different from her own. Eventually, they found a solution that supported their needs, both as separate people with a difference of opinion and as a couple who shared finances. They would pay half the vet bill and let the dachshund's owner pay the other half.

Once we really begin to listen to our partner in good faith — especially when we don't agree with her — we're on our way to a relationship based no longer on the struggle for control or self-protection but on the power of true connection.

Skill 2. Listening without Barriers

"My partner is too defensive." That's one of the most common complaints I hear from couples. There are several ways to define the term *defensive*. My favorite way is that of author Sharon Ellison. In her book *Taking the War out of Our Words*, she says that defensiveness is "reacting with a war mentality to a non-war issue." Why do we do it — harden our posture, draw in our breath, think up a stinging retort — before we even consider what the other person is saying?[2]

Our brain is wired for connection. When we begin to love someone, our connection circuitry lights up and dominates. We anticipate the best in our new partner, and we're rewarded, because each thing she says and does activates the connection center of our brain. We view her actions and intentions and interpret her language through the lens of our positive vision.[3] As the chemistry of love fades, a second kind of circuitry emerges. It turns out that we're wired for self-protection as well. When we experience our partner as a threat, we withdraw to protect ourselves from further injury. Withdrawal and disconnection are what continue to create trouble. At the heart of our vulnerability lies the feeling that we've lost our best friend. Our heart and body ache for her return. Yet often our behavior is the last thing that would invite her back.

On the Receiving End

Books on communication often emphasize the importance of expressing anger and complaints, but seldom do they tell us how to cope with being on the receiving end of them. How do you sit calmly and quietly while your partner describes you as stingy, selfish, moody, mouthy, or all of the above? What's the correct posture for listening to your lover lament that you're neither emotionally available nor trustworthy? How do you silence your inner lawyer's counterargument?

Your response to criticism depends on several factors: temperament, history, and self-esteem. Some people have nervous systems that respond more frequently and intensely to sensory stimulation. They may have a more exaggerated startle response than other people, even others in the same family. Often their bodies remain on high alert, and they are perpetually scanning the environment for danger. They may often hear themselves described as "too sensitive" or "thin-skinned." Such people, who are prone to defensiveness, may perceive an attack in certain situations in which people with resilient and calm temperaments would perceive none.

In addition, your childhood history has a lot to do with how you respond to complaints. If your parents shamed you often and punished you harshly it's likely that, as an adult, you quickly feel self-protective whenever you see someone upset and angry about something.

My client Jack grew up with an angry father who worked the

swing shift and slept in the mornings. When Jack was little, he and his siblings often woke their father accidentally as they got ready to go to school. Whenever they did, their dad would storm into their room and demand to know who had made the sound that woke him. The children blamed each other, and the unfortunate child singled out was yelled at and often hit. Jack learned early to assume that anger in another person meant, "Somebody's going to get hurt, and I'd better make sure it isn't me."

Later in life when Jack's partner, Daisy, began to grumble about something he'd said or done, he'd reflexively remind her of all the things she'd done wrong.

"Okay, so I forgot to tell you your sister called," Jack might say. "As forgetfulness goes, though, it's not half as bad as some of your mistakes. You left the stove on all night and ran up our electric bill. That's the kind of carelessness that will cause the house to burn down."

Daisy learned to withhold her negative feelings rather than express them openly. Yet this came at a high cost. Left unaddressed, her unmet needs surfaced indirectly and inappropriately. She "forgot" to pass on important information to Jack. She rolled her eyes when he told her about his troubles at work and then denied that her attitude was spiteful. Increasingly, she was less and less interested in physical closeness and sexual intimacy.

Reptiles for Brains

Whenever a threat is perceived, it registers in the old part of your brain, which some researchers refer to as reptilian. Your body is flooded with the neurotransmitters and hormones that alert you to danger and prepare you for battle. Once these chemicals are present, you can only comprehend a tiny fraction of what's going on. Just when your ability to see the whole picture shrinks, your certainty that you're right expands.

Say you're out hiking in the mountains. Suddenly you see a cougar moving slowly on the next ridge, stalking you. You don't stop to smell the wildflowers or wonder from what direction the cougar came. Your entire system focuses on how to escape or how to kill the cougar before it kills you. There's no room in the situation for anything but certainty and action.

Now, say you come home from a hard day, stressed and tired, and your partner is annoyed because you forgot to pick up groceries. If you're tired and cranky, the complaint may feel almost as threatening as the sight of the cougar. You might react as if you were fighting for your life. When you feel under attack, your body is flooded with warning chemicals. You have three options: to freeze, flee, or fight.

Forget the Groceries and Freeze

If you freeze, you'll sense your IQ dropping several points. Words elude you, and it feels impossible to decide what to do next. You act out the belief "If I'm quiet and don't draw attention, I'm less likely to get hurt." If you tend to freeze, you might deflect trouble with a plea for sympathy. Here's an example.

Your partner says, "Did you forget the groceries?"

You say, "Oh, gosh, I'm so sorry. I'm just not feeling well. I hope you're not mad."

Your partner replies, "I'm not mad, but I wish you'd remembered."

You say, "I've forgotten other things in the past few days. In fact, I'm worried that I may be running a fever."

You go lie down on the couch.

Forget the Groceries and Flee

If you tend to flee, most likely you're wired in such a way that, in the face of stressful conflict, your body wants to run to avoid entrapment and harm. This urge to bolt can take the form of denial of problems, procrastination, or withdrawal. When you flee, you act on the belief, "If I get away from you, and you can't catch me, then you can't hurt me." Here's an example.

Your partner says, "Did you forget the groceries?"

You reply, "Well, I thought we could make do with something light tonight. We could stand to eat less, you know."

Your partner says, "But we don't have any eggs, and you said you'd get some."

You say, "Look, I can't deal with this right now. I've got a lot of reports to finish tonight. I'll buy eggs tomorrow."

You shut the door to your study.

Forget the Groceries and Fight

Just like Jack, fighters believe that "the best offense is a good defense." And just as Jack did with Daisy, they deflect criticism through retaliation. They use the faults and transgressions of their "opponents" against them. The fighter experiences an apparent rise in IQ, and words come easily in the quest to offer proof against any complaint. Here's an example.

Your partner says, "Did you forget the groceries?"

You snap, "All I need today is your criticism."

Your partner replies, "I just asked a simple question."

You say, "With you, nothing is simple. It's always about what I do wrong. What about you? What about my birthday you forgot? What about Thursday, when you locked your keys in the car? Your brother always said you were an airhead."

You leave the room and slam the door.

Although we can't rewire ourselves to stop our initial primal reaction to freeze, flee, or fight, we can learn to override our first reaction and behave much more constructively. In the case of the groceries, for example, with some mental and emotional adjustment, we can learn to respond with something like "I'm sorry, I did forget them," and then offer to go to the store.

Often, our partner just needs to register disappointment and once he feels heard will respond with something like, "Hey, it's okay. I know you had a long day," and it's over. Or he may appreciate your going back out and getting the eggs. In any event, a small thing stays a small thing, because we've learned to override our initial inclination to freeze, flee, or fight.

Understanding Our Triggers

One of our challenges, then, is to understand the particular triggers that make us want to freeze, fight, or flee when we face potential conflict. Our work is to detect the filter that distorts the lens through which we see and hear our partner. If I expect to be criticized, I'll hear criticism in the most benign of remarks. If I assume that women are manipulative or that men are emotionally vacant, I'll find evidence to support my assumption before my partner has even formed words.

Imagine two switches that control the light in which we hear, understand, and respond. The first switch turns on a soft, warm light and is called "connection." When it's on, it intensifies the other colors in the room and makes us feel open and receptive. The second switch turns on a red light and is called "protection." It casts a fearful, angry shadow. Fear is useful: it warns us that there may be danger, and anger can give us the courage to act. The problem arises when the red light goes on at the same time for both people in an argument. When we feel threatened by the other's opinion, it's difficult to settle our system down again so that we can relax and reconnect.

One auxiliary skill that can help is self-soothing. This process allows us to calm down when we feel most upset until our emotional intensity subsides. If we remain calm, we'll be able to hear our partner out and not feel defensive or diminished while we listen. Remember, nobody can speak fairly or hear clearly when she's triggered. So how do we self-soothe?[4]

We don't wait for our partner to do something different, nor do we reach for a cookie or a glass of wine or distract ourselves by checking our email. Instead, we practice slow breathing and send ourselves positive messages that replace the repetitive negative thoughts about our partner. For example, we might notice what happens after we say to ourselves something like this: "If I could be curious about her reaction instead of defensive, I wonder what I might discover?"

With time and practice, we can learn to manage the anxiety that stems from our particular fears. Then when our partner presents us with something unwelcome, we can at least give it some consideration rather than instantly challenging and trying to squelch it. Once we listen long enough to understand our partner's point of view, we may find that our attitudes and opinions change substantially. Such conversations can lead to adjustments by both people, which in turn build harmony and intimacy.

Skill 3. Accepting Your Differences and Learning How to Collaborate

The research is clear: one of the primary differences between couples who thrive and those who dive is how they manage conflict. Couples who thrive are likely to possess two strong skills: they can see and accept their differences and, paradoxically, because of this ability, they can be generous and collaborate on a happy coexistence.

News anchor Diane Sawyer has said, "A good marriage is a contest of generosity." Easier said than done, of course. Neurobiologists suggest that some people are more genetically equipped than others to behave with generosity. Conversely, some people withhold more than others. Temperament isn't everything, but it does account for a lot. Yet we can learn to override our predisposition to some degree. At first we simply go through the motions and practice the new behavior, say, of generosity. Eventually, the feeling itself will follow. Although to be generous may never be our first instinct, it can feel far more natural in time.

I'll Never Be You

Paul and Brad sat before me in my office. It was their first therapy session, and they set out to describe the differences between them that made them both miserable. Paul went first: "I come from a family that likes to celebrate, so it feels pretty dismal to see my birthday come and go without any recognition from Brad." As he spoke, Paul slumped in his chair. Brad, meanwhile, sat upright, at attention. His face was a blank. I couldn't tell how he felt about his partner's complaints, which continued. "Plus, he has to control everything," Paul went on. "It's always got to be his choices: his restaurants, his movies, his concerts, and his vacation spots." He spoke quickly and, from time to time, glanced over to see how Brad was taking his words. But Brad gave nothing away and continued to sit beside Paul like a stone. His silence seemed to fluster Paul. "Don't get me wrong," Paul said, almost apologetically. "Brad has impeccable taste in everything, but that's not the point." He began to speak even faster, and the irritation in his voice mounted. "It's just that he never asks me what I want. He never says anything to show he cares, either. Not a word of endearment or appreciation." He turned to Brad: "I give to you in more ways than I can count. Why can't you give a little in return?" His agitation dissolved suddenly, and pain crept into his voice. "Why can't you be more openhearted, Brad?"

For the first time, Brad moved. He readjusted himself in his chair so that he could look at Paul. "Generosity comes so easily to you, Paul," he said. "It's like a giant doorway you pass through all the time. For me, though, it's a keyhole. I have to squeeze myself through it, and I only manage to do that every now and then."

Brad was calm when he spoke. His voice was soft, and he expressed no irritation. "I'll work on it and make a real effort," he said, "but I'll never be you, Paul." Then he turned to me and said, "Our friends call Paul 'the Heart.'"

Generous and, to use his own word, openhearted, Paul was passionate and intense in temperament, whereas Brad was calm and collected. As I got to know them better, it became evident that Paul was impatient with their differences in personality, whereas Brad was more accepting. He was aware that his remoteness and his need to be in control were hurtful to his partner. He was willing to work to make changes, but he also knew that generosity would never come easily to him, just as patience would never come easily to Paul.

Yet the differences in the personalities of these two men also helped them to support each other. At the beginning of our sessions together, Brad often seemed shut down. Then Paul would lean in and say something that would get a laugh out of him, and, amazingly — to me, at least — Brad would suddenly loosen up enough to participate. Paul was a high-strung guy, and during our sessions he would sometimes work himself into a frenzy. Then Brad would step in and, with a just few quiet words, help Paul relax.

Clearly these two people loved each other. Despite the friction between them, the opportunity was there for many meaningful exchanges that could make their lives more exciting and enjoyable than if their temperaments were more similar. But, of course, they couldn't collaborate until they accepted their differences. To accept their differences would mean that Paul and Brad would need to truly recognize that there was another person in their relationship — someone besides themselves.

Once we recognize that we're two different people, we can maintain some inkling of a viewpoint other than our own. Yes, we can still feel disappointment, hurt, and even outrage. Only now we also become more willing to cross the bridge into our partner's world instead of demanding that he or she cross into ours.

Even as we're connected, human beings are fundamentally separate from one another. The ability to grasp both these realities at the same time — which psychotherapists call "differentiation" — is one of the most important facets of intimacy and maturity. (We will explore this topic in more depth in chapter 9.)

In other words, I don't lose myself when I am close to you, and I can hold our intimacy within me even as I am experiencing my own independence and separateness. I can hear your sorrows without feeling sad, appreciate your joys without feeling jealous or threatened, and even hear your complaints about me without needing to correct, challenge, or try to change your mind. In his book *All You Need Is Love and Other Lies about Marriage*, Dr. John W. Jacobs observes: "In short, you know you have successfully differentiated when you can spend three days with your parents and feel like your adult self."[5]

Thus, Paul and Brad needed to search their hearts and souls deeply enough to recognize and respect their own feelings and needs. To distinguish themselves as individuals, they needed to stay in touch with their own inner nature, strengths, and weaknesses. They needed to be honest enough to challenge — and gentle enough to soothe — themselves.

They also needed to consider what was fair to ask of each other. No relationship can work if the balance always tips in favor of one person. To strike a healthy balance between self, other, and the partnership is the challenge of a lifetime. To the extent that partners are able to do these things, they heal themselves and become more whole. To try to fix each other is pure folly.

Partner Yoga

We must begin with what we already have within us. Then we must adopt an emotional practice that is akin to a good yoga practice. Slowly we stretch into what love asks of us: forgiveness, kindness, empathy, and deep, courageous self-examination. As we develop such self-awareness, we begin to catch ourselves when we fantasize about how our partner "should be," and we return to a fuller, more realistic vision of our mate.

In his Guided Mindfulness Meditation, Buddhist teacher and writer Jon Kabat-Zinn says, "Mindfulness means paying attention in a particular way; on purpose, in the present moment, and nonjudgmentally."[6] In other words, the future is a fantasy, the past is over, and our job is to stay focused on the very moment we are in.

When we use our relationship as a place to practice mindfulness, we become less reactive because we have slowed down our responses, allowing us to respond to what is actually happening rather than to our fears or fantasies about what it might mean. When we are in this open, accepting place, the usual distractions of hurt, anger, grudges, and longing no longer pull us away or create defenses and judgments against our partners. This gives them the space to be themselves, not who we want or imagine them to be. This allows safety to grow between our partners and ourselves.

This exercise was helpful to Brad. The formality of a practice allowed him to let his guard down, and he began to let Paul know how much he admired him. He stretched to put his feelings out there in the open. His efforts thrilled Paul. Here was outer confirmation of Brad's loyalty and love for him.

"I don't need you to say so all the time," Paul told him. "I love your silences and, yes, there's even charm in your aloofness. But when you make a point to let me know how you feel about me, I'm really touched."

For his part, Paul used the partner yoga exercise to practice techniques that helped him soothe himself so that he didn't need to lean so much on Brad for reassurance and comfort. He stretched to live in the moment, which reduced his anxiety level and, with it, the urge to rush and then to become impatient when things didn't get done as quickly as he liked.

Brad was impressed. It was a relief, he admitted, not to have to guide Paul through every crisis. He was happy to be "the Rock of Gibraltar," as Paul called him, but he wouldn't mind a break now and then. Besides, it was much better for Paul to be more self-reliant.

Collaboration, then, isn't just a question of how two people find a way to share a life. It's a question of how each partner carries out the individual work that will equip him or her to build a good life with another person. If we can slow down our first reactions and respond as lovers instead of fighters (or freeze-ers or flee-ers), we can create a relationship with more security and freedom for each of us. In turn, we can start to get creative. That's when collaboration gets exciting: we work off the sparks in each other to build something to serve us separately and together, the way that Paul and Brad were able to do. This kind of partner yoga helps us to reach for our best possibilities. In fact, it will help us to better connect with everyone in our lives.

Skill 4. Making a New Move

When we feel disappointed in love or worried in life, most of us move in one of two directions: either we shut down and push away, or we move closer to seek comfort and care. If you give in to your first instinct, however, it's pretty certain to cause trouble. Notice how each conversation about the groceries led to a dead end, whether the instinct was to freeze, flee, or fight. No resolution could be had, and no reconnection could occur. Each of these instinctive moves was designed by nature to help us respond to urgent danger and necessarily kept us from self-examination. In our most intimate relationships, however, our instinctual response is often the opposite of what our partner needs, and it's here that our willingness to make a new, counterinstinctual move is needed.

Ted thrived on social contact. Ellen was private and needed a lot of time by herself, especially when she was upset. When the couple suffered any kind of misunderstanding, Ted wanted to talk about it immediately, which made Ellen more anxious and apt to back away. Her distancing only increased Ted's distress, because he wanted to fix the problem immediately so that they could reconnect.

"Are you asleep?" Ted asked Ellen.

Earlier in the evening they'd had a stressful argument about a possible job switch that would require the couple to relocate.

"I need to sleep," Ellen said. "I don't want to talk now."

Ted couldn't understand how Ellen could sleep after they'd just had a fight — not if she really cared about the relationship. He got up and began to pace at the foot of the bed. "Come on, Ellen, you can sleep later. Right now we need to talk this problem through."

"Ted, can't you see I'm exhausted?" Ellen burrowed deeper under the covers to show him how much she wanted to go to sleep.

"That's insulting — don't you know that? — to turn your back on me when we're in the middle of something we need to resolve." Ted walked over and gave his wife's shoulder a gentle touch.

As soon as he touched her, she shot up in the bed and exploded. "Leave me alone," she screamed. "Just back off!" She jumped out of bed and went off to another room to sleep.

Ted was devastated. He wondered whether the marriage was over.

Ellen, meanwhile, felt great relief once she crawled into bed in their guest room down the hall. She fell asleep almost instantly.

This couple came to a class of mine with the knowledge that they had to change this pattern but with no clear idea how. It took them a short while to understand the concept of the counterinstinctual move, and with practice they were able to change their dynamic.

Still, whenever they have an argument, Ted's first instinct remains the same. If they are in bed he still wants to say, "Ellen, are you asleep? I'm feeling a need to talk about what happened between us."

Then he remembers that she is wired differently than he is. Instead of trying to initiate a conversation, he lies still and silently soothes himself. Just because Ellen is different from him doesn't mean she doesn't care about him and their marriage, he reminds himself. He breathes slowly until he can relax and not personalize her need for sleep before they talk again.

Occasionally, of course, Ted can't resist trying to reconnect quickly. Ellen will hear him ask, "Hey, you asleep?" But she no longer snaps, "I was until you woke me!" Although it's not her first instinct, she usually remembers to gently reach out and touch her husband's arm before saying, "Ted, I'm not ready to talk. How about we discuss this after work tomorrow?"

Each of them made a move that was counter to what came naturally: Ellen moved a little closer, and Ted moved away. As a result, the couple gradually managed to loosen and finally exit the endless loop they had been caught in so miserably. Each learned to see that the other's behavior wasn't wrong — just different — and both learned to stretch beyond their own comfort zone.

Skill 5. Nourishing the Relationship

Committing to an exercise program is easy when we're feeling energetic and inspired. What matters is what we do on those mornings when we don't want to drag ourselves to the gym. It works the same way in relationships. When all is going well, most of us find it easy to be generous, kind, and affirmative. When we perceive our partner to be the cause of our trouble, however, we must learn to counter our natural urge to punish, withhold, and otherwise flip into self-protection mode. Once we've learned to be less defensive, we can begin to choose our responses to disappointment and fear rather than giving in to the instinctive fight, flee, or freeze response.

One wise choice is to practice the Golden Rule, that moral truth honored by people of diverse cultures and faiths. Can I make a commitment to treat my partner as I would like to be treated? Can I respond to the situation in accordance with my highest spiritual values? If I were a loving person, how would I behave right now?

To make a practice of being kind and building goodwill doesn't mean setting no limits on our availability and generosity. It doesn't mean we never say no. Nor should it signal that we will accept mistreatment. It's not okay to break your word, be inconsiderate, or repeatedly ignore my needs.

At the same time, you can't force me to deploy the nuclear

weapons of hostile communication (such as sarcasm, blame, and bullying) in response to what you say and do — or don't say and don't do. Just because I set down boundaries gently in no way undermines their strength. I adopt this practice for me. If you're nasty and I get nastier, we succeed only in escalating the conflict. I don't win, and neither do you.

Remember, feelings aren't the only measure of love. The positive actions we take to override our instincts matter even more. If I can bring you a latte in the morning, fill your car with gas, and make your birthday special even when I'm annoyed with you, I'm funding the goodwill account of our relationship bank. If I can care for some of your needs, although they're different from mine, I can mine some of the gold in the relationship — the gift of seeing the other.

Particularly for those in the first throes of love, such conscious "bank deposits" may seem unnecessary. During the first stage, couples believe that nothing will pop their love bubble — ever. Yet to make such deposits is vital. From the very beginning, we need to nourish the relationship and keep the "love account" out of the red so that it can withstand some of the trouble to come, when we begin to appraise each other with cooler eyes and hearts. When we've stored up goodwill, we can recover much more quickly from hurt and distress than when we're running on empty.

Skill 6. Keeping Your Own Tank Filled

The ultimate nourishment we must provide is to the garden of our own well-being. To nurture our own creativity, friendships, mind, body, and spirit is equally important as caring for the relationship.

For years my husband and I had the same circular discussion.

We would finish teaching a five-day couples seminar, and as soon as the last person was out the door he would be changing into his biking clothes to go for a long, hard ride. Meanwhile, I would be sitting in the living room on my favorite couch wanting to go over the entire workshop with him, moment by moment. (He referred to this as a "postmortem.")

"Come for a ride with me," he'd say with slight irritation.

"After we talk about what just happened," I would bargain.

We would travel the same kind of loop on a Saturday morning after we had worked hard all week. He would rise early, a certain gleam in his eye and say, "Let's go for a long walk up Mary's Peak this morning."

"Tim," I would protest, "we've been working so hard this week. I don't want to see more people. I just want to lie in bed and read a book." This argument, in various forms, took place for decades until we figured out that each of us needed to do something different to find ourselves again. I recharge by going within, he by spending time with people or doing something active.

The more room I have to care for myself, the more I can bring to you. And when you're not available and I'm thrown back on my own company, I will have learned how to be with myself, not simply by myself. That ability is the taproot of relationship.

Chapter Four

DISILLUSIONMENT

There is no magic any more,
We meet as other people do,
You work no miracle for me
Nor I for you.

You were the wind and I the sea —
There is no splendor any more,
I have grown listless as the pool
Beside the shore.

But though the pool is safe from storm
And from the tide has found surcease,
It grows more bitter than the sea,
For all its peace.

— SARA TEASDALE, "After Love"

"Two souls, alas, are dwelling in my breast." In a single line of his heartrending play *Faust*, Goethe cuts straight to our human dilemma: the contrary yearnings that push and pull to find expression in our lives. Nowhere is this tug-of-war played out more fiercely than in our most intimate relationships.

Once we move from the doubt and denial of the second stage into the full-blown disillusionment of the third, we become even more aware of the contradictions seething within us. Part of us yearns to stay in committed connection, while another part longs to break free. This rebel side of us champions the independence that's at our core. Alongside our need for loving, each of us must nurture individuation, which Carl Jung defined as "the process by which a person becomes an 'in-dividual,'" that is, a separate and indivisible whole. Jung described this as "what makes a tree turn into a tree."[1]

Clearly, we need both "souls" within us at once: the one that can merge and the one that can stand apart. Our aim is to make peace, first between our two souls and then between ourselves and another person. It's quite a high-wire act, to learn to simultaneously love oneself, love another, and cultivate the space between the two, especially during tough times. It's reassuring to remember that our world is filled with opposing forces that nonetheless work in concert — light and shadow, stillness and activity, blooming and waning. With a lot of effort and a little bit of grace, we can learn to do the same.

Back to the Beginning

The dynamics of the third stage of love are much like those we encountered at the outset of our lives. If we were lucky, we started out cocooned with our mother or other caregiver in a blissfully merged stage. Somewhat later, as toddlers, we began to push away to explore a small portion of the larger world. After these brief forays, we scampered back to our parents to make sure they were still there for us. Once we found out that indeed they were, we pushed off again for more adventurous exploration.

As toddlers, we needed to assert ourselves yet remain connected. When we were in the throes of our so-called terrible twos, we weren't really so terrible after all. We were simply mired in the tension between conflicting desires — freedom and connection

— that we couldn't sort out; hence, howling tantrums in child-hood, and power struggles in our later relationships.[2]

Now, as adults, the same confusion and frustration trouble us during the stage of disillusionment. This time around, we try to act more like grown-ups. Our success is partial at best. Grow-ing our self has become more important than trying to foster our relationship; in fact, these processes often seem to be at odds.[3]

Love's Cold Interval

Disillusionment is the dark, wintry season of love. By now power struggles have risen fully to the surface. Passion may have gone missing. Emotionally estranged from our partner, we sense the distance between us lengthening by the minute. We have the same arguments over and over and are nearly worn out.

Some couples endure this phase quietly, managing to main-tain a thread of connection. Their attachment isn't interrupted, although their doubts feel very real. Others slog through it with a lot of drama, distress, and sometimes even violence. However expressed, this dip in love and trust is a part of most relationships. Amid the pain and the strife, it may be a stretch to see Disillu-sionment as a natural phase of love. But that's what it is — and more. Like every stage of love, this one offers us a gift, if we can muster the courage and patience to discover it.

When it comes to love, we have two primary tasks. One, as most of us know, is to learn to truly love another. The other task is less familiar but even more important, which is to learn how to love ourselves. Here I'm not talking about the type of self-regard that is really vanity, fed by money, power, influence, a gym-toned body, or the admiration of others. What I mean is the kind of love that leads to self-care — not only of our physical health but also of our minds and hearts. It's the kind of love that allows us the time to develop and use our talents. It's the kind of love that frees us to find and foster our true purposes in life.

It's a paradox: when we feel good about ourselves, we're more likely to feel generous toward others. We feel grounded and centered enough to take a risk and reach out. We feel safe enough to be flexible, acknowledge our shortcomings, and forget ourselves long enough to open up to our partner wholeheartedly. Often the people who have the hardest time making apologies have the meanest inner critics.[4] Loving ourselves doesn't mean that we're above criticism. It does mean that, imperfections notwithstanding, we hold a deep conviction of our own worthiness and our right to be treated with care and respect. If you take in only one message from this chapter, I hope it's this: *we need care and respect from ourselves even more than we do from our lovers.*

The Return of the "I"

In the first stage of love, you and your partner merged into a glorious illusion of oneness. In stage two, you awakened to your differences just long enough to panic, deny them, and cling to the "we." Now, in the third stage, clinging to fantasy is no longer an option. We've discovered that our differences are real, infuriating, and enduring. Profoundly disenchanted, each of us turns our back on the "we" and runs for cover to the perceived safety of "I." But to become truly wholehearted in our loving, we must integrate the two forces — the I and the we.

Just a few generations ago, the mark of a good marriage was its longevity. Other signs might have included having raised a reasonably happy and healthy family, or having achieved financial security and a comfortable retirement. Today things are very different. Emotional fulfillment is our number one marker of marital success, and we believe we have the right to long-lived intimacy and passion with our partner.

Yet to share this kind of love with another becomes possible only if we first experience it within ourselves. Perhaps not surprisingly, few of us achieve that state of inner care until long after the last drop of the love drug is gone. When the romance meds wear off, we're thrown back on our own resources. If we're wise, we'll hang out there for a while and take an honest, kind look at what we find.

It takes most of us a long time to look candidly at ourselves, partly because we become so obsessed with the faults of our partner and the generally distressed state of our relationship. Back in the first stage (how long ago that now seems!) we exaggerated the depth and breadth of the best qualities of our partner. Now, in the third stage, we flip-flop between attachment and disillusionment. *How unremittingly annoying he is! How outrageously self-centered she is!* Both extremes of viewpoint — *my partner is fabulous in all ways* and *my partner is worthless* — are gross distortions. Our challenge is to understand our seesawing hearts, and then to act from a more balanced place. That's the goal. Until we reach it, though, we may endure some trying times.

Over a Cliff

Eleven years into their relationship, Megan and Charlie appeared to fairly vibrate with success and well-being. Married and the parents of nine-year-old twins, they lived in Lake Oswego, an affluent suburb of Portland, Oregon. Fixtures at local charity functions, the two had a busy social life and charmed everyone in their wake. But beneath the glossy exterior, the couple was at war. Charlie's country upbringing used to fascinate Megan. Now she found many of his habits and attitudes uncouth. His wacky sense of humor still did her heart good privately, but his offbeat behavior got on her nerves socially. To keep her cool, she moved away from him at parties and other functions so she wouldn't have to watch him "make a fool of himself" again.

Megan made no effort to hide her contempt for qualities that Charlie felt were at his very core. "Farm humor," she'd often say, with a roll of her eyes or a shoulder shrug, after he told a story with a punch line or a funny ending, when they were at dinner with friends. Megan's put-downs hurt and infuriated Charlie, though he didn't object out loud. He liked to make people laugh. If that made him a clown, so what? He considered himself intelligent and reasonably well informed, if not an expert on the Czech Republic. Still, his idea of a fun get-together was not a reenactment of *Meet the Press* in their friends' living room.

Much as he hated to admit it, he'd come to notice how much more like her parents Megan was than he'd realized. He found her attachment to status very unattractive. Like her mother, she often treated waiters, salesclerks, and other service people rudely. Like her father, Megan loved to name-drop. The new people they met always learned quickly that Megan had an MBA from Harvard. *Give it a* rest, Charlie thought.

At home, their marital battleground had become the kitchen. Now a vegan, Megan struggled to tolerate Charlie's requirement for meat at nearly every meal. He always seemed to forget to use the red pots and pans that Megan had expressly marked for use by "carnivores." Charlie, meanwhile, watched his wife cut up all of her food into tiny pellets. She nibbled and chewed, just like a rabbit. This image stuck in his head no matter how diligently he tried to rid himself of it.

As far as Charlie could tell, Megan never relaxed. Now that

their babies had grown into children, her tendency to try to control every situation had reduced her to a kind of domestic cop. Years had passed since she'd praised him for being so wonderfully laid-back. Now she blew up when he neglected her to-do lists and just hung out with the kids on a Saturday afternoon. All he wanted to do was counter the children's nonstop schedule of activities during the week. Their regimen of homework, music lessons, and three kinds of sports swallowed all their time. Adults supervised them incessantly. Times of unstructured play in nature had defined Charlie's childhood, and he resented that his kids were not allowed to experience the freedom and wonder that had been so formative in his life.

Megan, meanwhile, considered herself fortunate in many realms, including her children and work. The only problem, she felt, was her poor choice of husband. What a slob Charlie had turned out to be! Straight off the farm. Once he'd sprawled out on their bedspread with his street shoes on and had left dirty footprints on the white silk. He left tiny whiskers in their bathroom sink after he shaved. She dreaded going out with him to restaurants, because he was always the loudest person in the room and made stupid jokes to waitresses. To Megan, these annoyances had come to define Charlie.

With little to say to each other anymore, the couple relied more and more on their social life. They entertained in their home regularly and were deft enough to keep even close friends unaware of just how hostile their marriage had become. On the rare weekend evenings that they had no plans, they sat stiffly in their living room, each mindful of the long list of hot topics to be avoided. They coped mostly by remaining silent or carrying on superficial conversations about the children's activities. Sex was infrequent and perfunctory at best.

The Turning Point

Every fall, Charlie drove to eastern Oregon to join his father and three brothers for an elk-hunting trip they had made together since he was seven years old. For an exhilarating week they camped and tracked in the wilderness, alternately sharing silence and reminiscing about their boyhoods. In his family, it was what fathers did with their sons. Fathers taught their boys how to go totally quiet, spot and stalk game, and become familiar and confident with their rifles. The boys learned respect for all creatures, including the hunted.

Ever since his son was born, Charlie had looked forward to the time when he would be old enough to learn the ways of the woods. When Ben turned seven, Charlie had broached the subject, but Megan wouldn't hear of it and closed off further discussion. Now that Ben was nine, Charlie believed that the time had finally come. Their son was more than ready to enjoy all that the hunting trip had to offer, and Charlie was hopeful that Megan would be more open to the idea. That, however, wasn't the case.

As they stood face-to-face in the living room, Megan began to list all the reasons why Ben shouldn't go. As was his habit under stress, Charlie locked his face into a smile. But his body told another story. He crossed his arms tightly across his chest and moved out of his wife's range, to stand behind his easy chair. After a few minutes, he realized he wasn't hearing most of what Megan was saying. Only certain phrases reached his ears: "insufficient precautions," "only nine years old," and "shooting defenseless animals."

The upshot: Megan refused to let Charlie take Ben hunting with his uncles and grandfather. Inwardly outraged, Charlie managed to keep his cool but could barely look at, let alone speak to, his wife. He vowed to himself that he would take the boy the following year, no matter what Megan said.

Once he joined his father and brothers out in the wilderness, Charlie unwound a little. But his anger and disappointment snuck up on him. He cataloged the misery he'd accumulated over the past several years. As he sat before the campfire one evening, a thought suddenly hit him: his marrying Megan had been a mistake, a huge mistake. It was time to face facts. They needed to call their marriage what it truly was — over. As he imagined his future freedom, he breathed a bit more evenly. He would still have his kids, at least part of the time. They could have fun together without Megan's perpetual nagging to "stop all this foolishness." Hell, he could even cook what he wanted in his own damn pots.

Then the shock of what he'd envisioned froze him mid-thought. Was this really the way he wanted things to go? Being a part-time father, having to tell everyone he'd failed? And then came the realization that he still cared deeply for Megan. That he yearned to find a way to touch — once again — those magic places between them. Did he really want to see his marriage dead and gone without a fight?

Charlie said good-bye to his dad and brothers the last night of the trip so he could leave well before sunrise and surprise Megan by coming home in the morning. On his way he stopped by an all-night market and bought several bunches of Megan's favorite flower, deep-blue Siberian iris. As he pulled into the driveway, he noticed that her car wasn't there. That was strange.

"Hello-o-o!" he bellowed as he walked into the kitchen. Silence. Where had everyone gone — to a soccer match at dawn?

Later, Charlie would learn that their yellow Lab had gotten violently ill during the night, and that Megan, the kids, and the dog had all rushed to the vet. For now, he placed one vase of irises in the foyer and took the rest of the flowers upstairs, where he set another vase on the desk that Megan used in their bedroom. As he positioned the vase, his gaze fell on an email printout, which lay on the desk, front and center. Maybe it explained where everybody had gone. He leaned down and read it: "Megan, I loved our night at the theater. Yes, it's complicated — but isn't love always? I will see you very soon. — James."

Chapter Five

SEVEN NORMAL TROUBLES

For relationships, too, must be like islands. One must accept them
for what they are here and now, within their limits — islands surrounded
and interrupted by the sea, continuously visited and abandoned
by the tides. One must accept the serenity of the winged life,
of ebb and flow, of intermittency.

ANNE MORROW LINDBERGH, *Gift from the Sea*

When we're in the disheartening throes of
Disillusionment, it's easy to feel that we're the only ones who
suffer grave disappointment. Other couples seem happy enough,
at least at a distance. Given my work with hundreds and hundreds of couples in therapy, however, I can say with confidence
that a number of predictable troubles befall most long-term part-
nerships. As hopeless as these woes may feel now, I promise that
you can learn to overcome them.

Two points emerge from our troubles during this third stage.
The first is the incorrect belief that our happiness and the success
of the relationship are determined by what our partner says and
does. As I've emphasized before and will again, *all relationship
change begins within you*. Once you shift your focus from your

partner to yourself, you gain enormous power to affect both your relationship and your own well-being. The second point is that many of the difficulties — both small and large — that we face in the third stage can't be resolved until we put serious time and energy into our partnership. We need to place top priority on nourishing the garden of our relationship.

These two points are well worth bearing in mind, given the seven normal troubles that couples tend to encounter during stage three. Let's take a look at each of them.

The Blahs

Life is predictable. Many of us trudge through our nine-to-five jobs only to come home to face the repetitive tasks of our personal lives — paying bills, putting together dinner, and perhaps settling in for an evening of mindless conversation or even bickering with our partner. The sheer tedium of it all can wear us down.

I live in Oregon, where the winters aren't white with snow and ice. Our winters are gray with rain, which may pour or drizzle but rarely ever stops. I keep framed photographs of spring flowers on my desktop to remind my clients and me that winter is temporary. Marital blahs can be temporary, too, if we learn how to recognize them and manage ourselves through the darkness.

The physiological explanation for the blahs is based on the human craving for pleasure. The feel-good chemical, dopamine, is released when our minds are excited and stimulated, and we feel off-balance when we experience a shortage. By the time we enter the third love stage, a good hit of dopamine can be hard to come by.

The biggest challenge of the blahs is not to blame our partner for the way we feel. Instead, we need to look for ways to accept the ordinariness of life, even as we respect the mind's natural craving for stimuli. The next challenge is to consider some steps we might take to add some healthy pizzazz to our daily grind — and then try out a few of them.

The Blues

If the blahs grip us for too long, we can sink into the blues. Many things can trigger depression, including genetic makeup, life crises, and the multiple disappointments that attend Disillusionment. Unlike medical conditions that can be diagnosed through measurable tests, depression is diagnosed through behavioral symptoms: exhaustion, a low sex drive, disturbed sleep, anxiety, reduced self-esteem, irritability, negativity, and a quicker-than-usual temper.

Often depressed people don't consider their problem an illness. They believe that they can simply will themselves out of the darkness. Others numb their pain temporarily with various forms of self-medication, including drugs, alcohol, sex, food, constant exercise, or long hours at the office. In our search for logical reasons for why we feel so pessimistic, apathetic, and easily frustrated, we often look to our imperfect marriage. That, we may decide, is the problem.

Countless studies point to depression as a major factor in unhappy marriages. In some cases, preexisting depression contributes to marital problems in the third stage; in others, the troubled relationship itself spurs depression. Often the two feed each other. In any event, depression is exhausting. Life with a depressed partner is exhausting, too, especially when we try to "fix" our partner's problem.[1] Compassion fatigue runs high, and our tolerance runs low. A depressed person needs to seek a health-care professional for diagnosis and treatment, just as he would for any other illness.

Betrayal

Betrayal can take many forms, from garden-variety lapses in judgment to genuine heartbreakers and marriage breakers. Many such lapses can be avoided if we take the time to pay attention to what our partner's world really feels like. What does your partner need to feel comfortable and safe? Be aware that what he or she needs may be very different from what you need.

George, who owns a restaurant, is a raconteur and an open book. He excels at sharing anecdotes and recounts whatever is going on in his life with everyone — friends, employees, gas station and parking lot attendants, the tellers at the local bank, even fellow riders in the elevator.

George's wife, Sarah, is reserved and private. A poet, she is serious, contemplative, and in need of a great deal of solitude. These needs complement his own. After long, hard hours at the restaurant, George is glad to go home to Sarah's tranquil oasis.

Sarah admires and relies on George's zest and wit. George makes her laugh and allows her to take life less seriously. Still, Sarah wants him to respect her privacy. Countless times she's told him, "Just leave me out of your stories."

Recently, Sarah learned that she was a finalist for a prestigious national prize for poetry. Thrilled and excited, she called George at the restaurant as soon as she opened the envelope.

"That's fantastic, Sarah. I'll bring home champagne."

"Oh, don't bother," she demurred. "It's not like I've won anything."

"Sure it is. It's a huge honor to be a finalist. We'll celebrate!"

"All right," Sarah relented. "You know I love champagne."

No sooner did George get off the phone than he shared the news with the staff in the kitchen and patrons out in the dining room. "Looks like my wife just won a big prize for poetry," he crowed. "Well, she's in the running, anyway."

Late that night at home, George poured two flutes of champagne. "Here's to my clever wife, the poet."

"Thank you, but I haven't actually won anything," Sarah reminded him again.

"Yes, you have! It's the recognition you deserve. The kitchen staff is all excited. They're going to bake you a congratulations cake."

After a small silence, Sarah whispered, "You *told* them?"

"Of course. Why not?"

"Because I asked you not to, that's why." Sarah was livid. "You'd think I'd know better by now! You're the last person on earth I should tell anything to. There's no censor in your mind, you don't think before you speak. You're just thoughtless."

George was bewildered. In his view, being named a finalist for the award was an honor. But that wasn't how she saw it. She dreaded the thought that all these people would find out that she was an also-ran.

George just shook his head. How could his wife be angry with him about something he'd done out of love and pride? Clearly, he was the victim here.

In fact, George *was* guilty of something. He saw the extent of his wife's need for privacy as unreasonable, so he simply disregarded it. "Why aren't you me?" That was the question at the heart of this conflict.

Other common forms of betrayal include lies, broken promises, sexual unfaithfulness, financial deception, and the invasion of privacy — from snooping on a computer to reading a private journal. When the breach of faith is exposed, the betrayed person may come to question everything about her partner and the relationship itself. Beyond the inevitable shock, anger, and hurt, betrayal often leaves its victims with a grievous loss of self-worth.

Those who betray their partners tend to rely on "reasonable" explanations to justify themselves. The reason they were unfaithful? Not enough sex in their marriage. The reason they maxed out the credit cards? Simple generosity — they wanted to take their partner on a first-class vacation. In truth, however, an act of betrayal is an act against the self, which harms a person's sense of integrity and self-respect. After betrayers digest what they've done and the pain they've caused, their shame and guilt can be all-consuming.

Because of its powerful reverberations for both partners, sexual betrayal is an especially difficult marital problem to cope with and resolve. Sometimes the only way to reconcile is for both partners to clean their respective psychological closets of all baggage and to reach down into the depths of those emotional storage vaults to find the courage, honesty, and love to repair and forgive. It's extremely hard work. But perhaps the depth of this process explains why some of the strongest marriages I know have arisen from extremely serious betrayals.

Lumpy-Carpet Syndrome

Conflict is part of every relationship. Yet many couples believe that strong differences of opinion mean that their marriage is troubled. Because none of us wants a troubled marriage, we tend to pretend we agree even when we don't. What we get is lumpy-carpet syndrome (discussed in chapter 2), in which we sweep under the rug the tensions that accompany our unspoken conflicts.

By the time we enter the third stage, the carpet has usually become very lumpy indeed, and we have to navigate carefully to find the few remaining smooth spots. It becomes increasingly difficult to cross the rug toward each other.

When we finally do face up to our differences, we must tread carefully. To let loose with whatever we think and feel is rarely an effective way to "de-lump" a carpet. Successful conflict management tends to be counterintuitive. It means listening to uncomfortable things that our partner may have to say about us. It means stretching to understand our own part in the conflict. It means speaking in a way that our partner can hear. These behaviors take considerable courage, patience, self-awareness, and practice. Yet all of us can — and must — learn these skills in order to restore trust and intimacy.

Loss of Connection

I sat in my office with Annie and Jane, two women on the verge of a breakup. It wasn't their complaints about each other that startled me. It was the moment that Annie put her head in her hands and sobbed, "I'm losing my best friend." Suddenly it became clear: the depth of her agony arose from the threat she felt her grievances posed to their existence as a couple.

When Annie forgot to pick up the dry cleaning, it wasn't Jane's biting sarcasm that upset her. It was the fear that what lay beneath Jane's annoyance was a profound disappointment in Annie. "She doesn't see me the way she once did," Annie cried.

Many of us erroneously jump to the conclusion that once we lose our idealized version of each other we will lose the relationship.

As noted in an earlier chapter, we're wired in our brains and hearts to be connected with others; numerous studies show that touching, hugging, and being a part of loving relationships helps us to live longer, healthier, and happier lives. So how can we manage the anger and conflict that are part of all relationships and avoid the loss of life-enhancing connection?[2]

Ironically, our first instinct may be to protest by criticizing and blaming our partner. Our flawed logic works something like this: "If you don't love me the way I need you to, I will punish you by ignoring or criticizing you, which will cause you to fall in love with me all over again."

Needless to say, this rarely works. Love is a feeling: it comes and goes, but constant criticism, sarcasm, and blame truly can threaten fundamental connection and lead to breakup.

The secret to keeping our relationship strong under duress is to manage our love account just as we manage our bank account — by keeping the deposits higher than the withdrawals. Listen, support, touch, apologize, appreciate, and surprise. (See skill 5, nurturing the relationship, one of the six skills discussed in chapter 3.) We need to practice these behaviors often enough to amass the goodwill to cover those times when the relationship is "overdrawn."[3]

We can be angry, hurt, outraged. It doesn't mean we cut off connection. It doesn't mean we fail to see the merit of our partner's main strengths. Although it may feel like the last thing we want to do, if we keep the bridge open between us, we'll find the way forward in the most difficult times.

Righteous Indignation

This trouble is a sneaky one and usually catches us totally by surprise. When Donna and her partner, Jon, moved into their new home, they were delighted with their spacious backyard, if no longer with each other. Given their disillusionment with the grandness of their love affair, the focus on home improvement was a diversion each of them welcomed.

A landscape gardener by trade, Jon decided to install a pond. He planted a beautiful array of ferns, lilies, and grasses to surround the koi and goldfish. When some neighbors came by to admire the pond, they cautioned that raccoons had come into the area lately and were likely to do some damage. Donna was concerned, but Jon assured her that he'd rework the landscape to create some deterrents. Then he got busy with clients and put off the antiraccoon project.

As the weeks went by, Donna urged Jon to do something to ward off the masked invaders. She even offered to hire someone else to do the work.

"You don't have to control everything," Jon snapped. "I'll get to it."

Donna said nothing more, but she resented Jon's procrastination. Bitterly, she prepared herself for the worst-case scenario. A week later, she awoke to backyard devastation. Lilies had been pulled up, dead fish flung about, holes eaten in the pond liner, and most of the water drained. Although she was saddened and horrified, she also was aware of a surge of righteous indignation as she marched into the house to wake Jon with the news. Donna felt almost giddy with satisfaction, intoxicated by the proof that she had been right. "What did I tell you?" she said, lording it over Jon.

Donna's reaction points to a trap that many of us fall into. She used this mistake her partner had made as an opportunity to vent her spleen about all sorts of grievances and resentments that had piled up and had nothing to do with raccoons or backyard ponds. The key that unlocked the floodgates of Donna's rage was that *she was in the right*: Jon really had screwed up, which gave her license to criticize him. She felt something like moral superiority as she gazed out the back window at the havoc on their property.

"What an idiot," she hissed.

"Excuse me, what did you say?" Jon asked. He was grappling with his own bitterness about the deterioration in his relationship with Donna, and when he looked out at the once-lovely pond and surrounding landscape, it seemed a perfect illustration of what had happened to them as a couple.

Donna turned to the man she once admired more than anyone else in the world and repeated what she'd said just a moment ago under her breath. Now there was triumph and contempt in her voice. As if she were the judge and Jon were the lowly convict on trial, she looked him in the eye and pronounced, "I said you were an idiot. And you are."

Jon barely grunted in response. Donna's attitude didn't surprise him. He no longer expected to receive kindness from her.

In the first throes of love, when we decide that we've met our soul mate, we leap at whatever stray evidence supports our joy and ignore anything that might signal trouble ahead. Now, in the third stage, just about everything our partner says or does can be interpreted as evidence that he doesn't know us, doesn't care about us, and isn't right for us. At this point both Donna and Jon saw signs of their failure everywhere. It would take a major restoration effort on their part to put things right in their lives together, never mind their garden.

Bad Moods

As an old English saying has it, "One day you're a peacock; the next day you're a feather duster." On peacock days, when everything is going our way, it's easy to behave lovingly. It's a snap to keep our promises to our partner. It's easy to allow disappointments and flashes of anger to subside and to move quickly to repair.

On feather duster days, none of this is easy. Sometimes, when life isn't going well, we simply find ourselves in a bad mood. This is perfectly normal. What matters is how we handle our bouts of grumpiness. Ask yourself how a bad mood affects your work performance. How do you treat your colleagues and customers? Now ask yourself: How do I treat my partner? My guess is that you stretch yourself so as not to indulge the bad mood at work, whereas at home you may make less of an effort.

If we surrender to bad moods in our relationship, we may experience some serious fallout. We may break our word or fail to show up. We may lash out and upset — or even abuse — our partner. What's called for, instead, is sticking with the program. If you want to create trust and good health in your relationship, you need to keep your word and your manners intact, even when you're feeling low. Psychologist Harriet Lerner, author of *Marriage Rules*, reflected on this topic in a recent Facebook posting: "I seem to be thinking about kindness this week. Something I appreciate more, the older I get. Of course, it's hardest to practice kindness with a spouse or family member. It's easier to practice kindness with your dry cleaner. We should practice wherever and with whomever we can. And we might also consider if we really want to treat our partner less well than we treat our dry cleaner."[4]

Words to live by — or at least to aspire to.

Chapter Six

DECISION

Don't search for the answers, which could not be given
to you now, because you would not be able to live them.
And the point is to live everything. Live the questions now.
Perhaps then, someday far in the future, you will gradually,
without even noticing it, live your way into the answer.

— RAINER MARIA RILKE, *Letters to a Young Poet*

If you stay together long enough, you're likely to
hit a wall — the hard, unyielding place you encounter when you
conclude that you and your partner differ in fundamental, intol-
erable ways. It seems there is no way forward — at least none
that you can make out. Your differences seem too intractable,
and you can't bear to struggle fruitlessly over the same issues
any longer.

Welcome to the fourth stage of love — Decision. By the
time you get here, you're probably pretty worn out. You've been
on this grim trek with your partner for so long. Maybe it's been
years, or maybe it just feels that way. In any case, you've slogged
through so much disappointment and teeth-grinding anger that

you're way past disillusion. You feel downright desperate. You realize that your life can't go on like this anymore.

Once you come to this conclusion, however, you haven't reached the end point. You've only come to a crossroads. You have many more decisions ahead of you. At this stage, caution is prudent, though it's probably the last thing you're in the mood for. You've been carrying so much pent-up emotion inside. Why not make a bold move and break loose from your insufferable partner, at last?

Your impulse to bolt is perfectly understandable. But years of work with couples has taught me this: you should not give in to the desire to make an immediate change, unless you are in danger. (If you are, then yes, make a move immediately.) If you're wise, you'll stop and ask yourself many questions before you take your next step. It's much smarter — and in your best interests, really — to slow down, at least long enough to understand how you got to where you are.

The fourth stage may seem like an awfully dismal place to linger. The conflicts are stark, the quarrels cause pain, and the boredom of the "same old, same old" may set your teeth on edge. The last thing you're inclined to consider is that you've reached a threshold rather than an impasse. But a threshold it is. You've arrived at a platform on which to rest, contemplate your choices, and possibly launch yourself into a life more exhilarating than ever before. Here, in this swampy morass, you may discover opportunities for renewal and growth.

You fell in love without effort, which is why it's called "falling." There was nothing you needed to do. You became disillusioned in the same way; think of how often people refer to "falling *out* of love." Now that you're played out, you're ready to wake up. In the fourth stage you've finally arrived at a place where you get to be in charge. You get to choose — really choose

— what to do next. It's not the decision you make that matters most, however. It's *how* you make your choice.

Step into Dilemma

The "how" of your choice is vital, because just after the realization hits — *I can't go on like this anymore* — few of us are in a position to make a good decision about the future of our relationship. Actually, most of us feel some ambivalence about the next step. Then we start to feel a little crazy about our conflicting urges. To stay feels impossible. To leave feels worse. What to do?

I'll say it once again: do *not* make irrevocable decisions at this point. In my experience, the wisest initial action is to step into the dilemma and accept it until the next step becomes very clear.

As Carl Jung observed in his article "Stages of Life," "we cannot live the afternoon of life according to the program of life's morning, for what was great in the morning will be little at evening, and what in the morning was true will at evening have become a lie."[1]

In the world of relationship, this means that the kind of love and friendship I needed at age nineteen won't be the same as what I need now, at forty-nine. Your definition of intimacy and support will be different, too. Just as a job contract needs review and revision over time, so does a relationship. This latter kind of review, however, requires courage, introspection, and the willingness to leave our comfort zone — the zone in which we shelter the story of who we think we are and how we got to where we are in our relationship.

As you perform your relationship review, you may be surprised to realize that some of your pain isn't caused by your partner, or even by the infinity loops described earlier, in which you're caught in the coils of painful and seemingly endless reactions and counterreactions. The hard truth is that your relationship with another person can't save you from loneliness, disappointment, and the impermanence of life. If you blame the relationship for not fulfilling you, you'll miss the real quest, which lies within. Ultimately, we make our journey alone.

If you take the time now to come to terms honestly with your motivations, your regrets and mistakes, and your needs and desires, you'll be much better equipped to assess your options and make a wise decision about your relationship. What you can learn about yourself in this stage will serve you well, whether or not you stay with your partner. Later in the chapter I will describe this process in more detail in a section called "Our Inner Quest."

Options and Outcomes

In this fourth stage, most couples choose one of four options: (1) to separate; (2) to stay and do nothing, remaining stuck in conflict or indifference; (3) to lead parallel lives; or (4) to rebuild and create a new, more rewarding partnership.

Regardless of which decision we make, we're left with unfinished business if we make it too quickly. If we leave the relationship without fully exploring and coming to grips with our own role in the conflict, we'll probably choose the same kind of person and re-create the same kind of problems all over again. If we stay together with bitterness and disappointment, our relationship will be nothing but an empty (and miserable) shell, unless we find a new source of energy to fuel a new kind of bond. If we remain a committed couple and want a better relationship, we can't return to our first, idyllic merge. We must create a new, healthier relationship, one that embraces both reality and possibility. To do that, we move into the fifth stage, Wholehearted Loving, which we'll explore a bit later.

Hard Decisions

Many couples stay together even when it hurts. They wage the same battles over and over, unable or unwilling either to leave or to change. This choice has a steep downside. Unhappy lives are toxic, and the personal costs to health and happiness are enormous. As the old saying goes, "if you always do what you've always done, you'll always get what you've always got."

But most relationships — even harmful ones — have positive elements, often making the decision to stay or leave a complicated one. The marital tumult that some of us endure reminds me of Duane, a client of mine, who was under court order to attend counseling sessions because of his record of domestic violence. His file was thick with trouble: not just violence at home but also driving while intoxicated and drug abuse.

Before our court-ordered sessions began, I invited in his wife, Charlene, for a meeting. A petite, thoughtful woman, she was candid about how much suffering she had experienced in her marriage and her doubts now about what the future might hold. "I love him," she told me, "but I fear that my love isn't enough to heal a lifetime of rage and hurt."

I was impressed with Charlene's openness and her realistic assessment of how little she could do to change her husband. This left me wondering: How could such a discerning person have chosen such an unappealing man in the first place?

The first time Duane swaggered into my office, he met me with a scowl. Dressed from head to toe in denim, he gave off a strong smell of stale cigarettes and diesel fuel. I quickly learned that his childhood had been brutal: both his parents were hard drinkers, and physical violence was an everyday occurrence. By age fifteen, he'd left home. Eventually, he found work at a mill and settled in a small Oregon town, where he met Charlene.

Although I did my best to look interested and professional, I counted the minutes until the first session with Duane was over. I wanted to open the windows and turn on the fan to remove any traces of him from my consulting room. I wondered how I could help someone whom I found so offensive and who showed no remorse, let alone any desire to change.

We spent the next few sessions stuck in our opposing views of each other. He was there to "take his counseling," and I was there to provide "anger management."

Then the day came when I happened to look out the window just before we were scheduled to meet. Duane had found a parking space just outside my office, and I noticed that his truck had a gun mount. No surprise there: I just *knew* he'd be a man who hunted for the fun of it.

When I mentioned the gun rack, he said, "Well, ma'am, I don't really like to kill things."

"If you don't hunt," I asked, "then why the gun rack?"

"'Cuz I need an excuse to get out to the woods and hear the loons."

"Loons? What loons?"

Duane looked up, genuinely startled. He pointed to the framed diplomas on my wall. "I don't mean no disrespect, ma'am, but what good is these degrees if you don't know about loons? They're the sweetest things the good Lord ever put on this earth."

I was touched by the gentle way he described the birds. I looked over at Duane, and for the first time our eyes really met. I noticed how beautiful his were, a vivid lake-blue. Somewhat shyly, he smiled.

"Loons," he went on, "may seem ordinary, like ducks and seabirds. But, Lord almighty, the way they call, there's nothing like it in God's whole world."

I no longer saw a scruffy, angry guy whose hygiene habits offended me. Here was a man who had found a piece of his soul in the woods. For the first time, I could see what Charlene saw in him.

Duane and I went to work. Slowly, he began to look at his behavior toward his wife and to acknowledge how wrong it was. I became convinced that he genuinely wanted to change. At the end of our final session, Duane said he had to go get something out of his truck.

When he returned, he nervously handed me a package wrapped in newspaper. "For you," he said. Inside was a circular metal saw.

On one side of the saw were two loons on a green lake. One sat on a log and gazed serenely across the water. The other had its wings spread in flight.

"I painted it so you could see the loons yourself," he said.

"Thank you," I managed to gasp, given how stunned I was that Duane had created something so delicate in its beauty.

He seemed to understand my appreciation. "Well, you taught me something," he said, "and I taught you something, and there ain't much more two people can do for each other." With a nod, he turned and left my office.

Duane was right: I had learned from him. I'd learned that I'd been much too quick to judge a very complex man. I kept that painted saw on a wall in my office for a long time. It reminded me that every human being holds mysteries and multitudes.

Sadly, Duane wasn't able to hold on to the insights and resolve that he'd gained during our sessions. After a brief period of sobriety and calm, he resumed drinking, fighting, and wreaking havoc on Charlene's life and the lives of others around him. One final, violent scene sent Charlene packing.

One of the gifts that the fourth stage can bestow is the clarity to see what's true. Potential for both health and self-destruction can lie side-by-side in the same human being. Charlene saw this duality, assessed her deepest needs, and made her decision. I could see why she loved Duane, and I could also see why she left him.

If You Leave

In his book *A Path with Heart*, Jack Kornfield writes that there are three questions someone asks themselves at the time of their death: "Did I love well?" "Did I live fully?" "Did I learn to let go?"[2]

He's right. Nonetheless, letting go is likely to be agonizing, whether we do it for reasons of physical safety or emotional survival, or simply because the vows we made at twenty-five no longer suit the person we are at fifty. When we leave a relationship, and for a time afterward, we will experience most of the following emotions.

Grief

No matter how certain you are that your relationship is over, you may feel a hole in your heart when you decide to leave. You are saying good-bye not just to your partner but also to a part of yourself — the part that began this relationship full of hope, trust, and tenderness. It's natural to mourn the loss of a dream. If you move through the separation or divorce process without grief, it's probably because you've already grieved for years, whether or not you were aware of it.

Anger and Blame

Anger is a normal and necessary emotion. It almost always accompanies loss, or the fear of loss. It helps us pay attention to a painful situation and gives us the energy to do what we can to change it. We need to feel it, acknowledge it, get the news it is telling us, act on it, and then move on.

If we feel powerless to make the change we want in our relationship, or if we feel victimized by another, we may get lost in blame, which is the handmaiden to anger. Blaming our ex-partner is a common reaction to the demise of a relationship. As Buddhist teacher and author Pema Chödrön observes, "Blaming is a way to protect your heart, trying to protect what is soft and open and tender in yourself. Rather than own that pain, we scramble to find some comfortable ground."[3]

In other words, we use blame as a crutch. We use it to justify the breakup without looking closely at the underlying reasons for it, which may be too painful to bear. Say, for example, that our partner is the one who has decided to leave. It's much easier to condemn him or her as the problem in the story than to confront our own part in its ending. It's also easier to justify our decision to split if we identify the cause as something wrong with the other person. Blame is tempting. But it's a little like ice cream or wine: a small amount can soothe, but too much can make you miserable.

In truth, it's quite possible that neither of you is any more at fault than the other. The end of the relationship is a sad outcome in a world that doesn't always deliver what we want. Acceptance of life's sorrows is the work of the adult. Over time, you may begin to look differently at your loss. As psychoanalyst Ethel Person observes, "People should not judge failed love affairs as failed experiences but as part of the growth process. Something does not have to end well for it to have been one of the most valuable experiences of a lifetime."[4]

Making Different Decisions

For better or worse, you and your partner are unlikely to cycle through love always in tandem or to reach the same decision about what to do next. Each of us is unique and sets out on our own path, no matter how merged we may feel with another at times. Given our distinctiveness, it's only natural that we travel at different speeds and sometimes find ourselves at a distance from each other. You, for example, may still feel merged with your lover, while he no longer feels the same dizzying passion you shared at the start. Or maybe she has reached the point of wholeheartedness, open to you without reservation. You, meanwhile, remain sunk in doubt.

To recognize the fundamental distance between any two human beings is especially important when we find ourselves at cross-purposes: when what we want is not forthcoming and may never be. Let's say that I love you more than you love me. That's just how it is. Now what?

It might be tempting for me to try to manipulate or bully you into loving me exactly the way I want you to. But I'd be operating on a false premise — that I have the power to change or control you. My only power lies in my ability to act on what is true for me. Can I thrive in this relationship the way it is, or not? My only decision is whether to stay in the relationship as it is.

And sometimes, just as we decide we are ready to do the work to make the relationship the best it can be, our partner decides she wants out. Once again, we have no control over her decision. What we can do is practice something that I call "soul care."

Soul care means that we continue to live our deepest values

even when we are in pain. Can we continue to be generous to our former partner — to wish her well at best and not wish her harm at least — despite the pain we believe she's caused us? Can we take on an even more difficult challenge, which is to recognize our part of the mess?

As much as I might resent this advice if I were experiencing the outrage that comes with feeling dumped, and in spite of my resistance to giving up my virtuous sense of hurt (because there is something soothing and satisfying about righteous fury, especially if we can get our friends to turn on our partner, too), I would want to remember one thing. There is a purely practical reason for giving up blame: it will release us from pain a lot sooner! Holding a grudge and fanning the flames of blame and resentment are often compared to drinking poison in the hopes that it will harm someone else.

In her memoir *This Is Not the Story You Think It Is*, novelist Laura Munson has written about the daunting challenge she experienced when her husband of two decades went through a personal crisis and wanted to end the marriage. Rather than react to his decision to leave with criticism or attack, she was able to separate her needs and desires from her husband's. (This was after she recovered from what felt "like a speeding fist, like a sucker punch."[5]) She remained clear that she did not want to part even though he did and stayed true to her wish to remain married. Although she sometimes raged and stormed internally, she didn't retaliate or beg him to change his mind. She gave him distance, she did the things that nourished her and the kids, and she worked very hard not to personalize his words. "It wasn't a strategy to stay married," she said. "It was a philosophy to stay healthy."[6]

Munson goes on to describe the importance of living her own truth about the marriage rather than being reactive to his: "If that time of my life had ended in divorce, I'd still consider it one of the most powerful times I've known.... Letting go of the future is a very powerful concept, and an even more powerful practice."[7]

What we make of our lives, then, is an inside job. Regardless of how our partner reacts or what decisions he or she makes, we are in charge of our own souls. What we nourish and cultivate within ourselves is what we can rely on. The qualities we nurture will prepare us either to stay mired in the past or to embrace a wealth of possibilities for the future.

Parallel Lives

Some couples decide to stay together, even though they no longer seek intimacy or share many of the same goals. Under one roof, they opt to lead parallel lives. This kind of relationship doesn't have to be empty. If two people are willing to accept the limitations of such a partnership and expand their systems of support, they may find comfort and support in such an arrangement.

In the latter part of the twentieth century, much emphasis was placed on finding a soul mate with whom we would share enduring, unconditional love. As a result, many people left "good-enough" marriages in search of the holy grail of romance and intimacy. Like many desperados, they never arrived at their destination but instead found themselves poorer in both pocket and spirit.

To describe a marriage or a partnership as good enough isn't to say that you should settle for something that makes you unhappy. A good-enough partnership is not one in which you pass your lives together in stony silence, stuck in resentful dreams of what might've been. Nor is it one in which your gut instinct says you need to leave, or when hostility and mean-spiritedness are the prevailing winds of the home atmosphere. In those cases, it is better to leave: a life lived alone can be liberating, one in which you find out how to be with yourself rather than by yourself.

That said, some marriages work well with minimal sizzle but enough mutual respect and kindness to support both parties. For some, a sense of allegiance is at the core of the partnership, and this loyalty can, in turn, anchor each individual's sense of well-being. For others, personal values, religious convictions, or simply the realization that one is likely to do better inside the marriage than outside it are all good-enough reasons to make the choice to stay. To succeed, however, this kind of marriage needs to be negotiated and then fine-tuned like any other, although the needs and expectations are quite different. One couple I know offers a good example of how such a marriage can work.

Keeping It Vital

Marge and Fred met in the Peace Corps. They had much in common — scientific interests and a commitment to making the world a better place — and they fell into an easy companionship. After they finished their service, marriage seemed to be the natural next step, although romance barely figured into their mutual affection.

Back in the United States, the couple went to graduate school and settled into a small academic community, where they have lived for nearly thirty-five years. As a professor of marine ecology, Marge studies coral reefs. She has spent many summers in Australia, where she learned to body-surf and body-build. As she approached her sixtieth birthday, she had never felt fitter.

Fred is an expert on forestry but spends most of his time behind a desk, where he writes articles, books, and grant proposals. Through the years, he has gained more than forty pounds and takes medication for high blood pressure.

Although their sex life fizzled early on in their marriage, their respective professional lives soared, which led them to spend less and less time in each other's company. Now, with retirement just a few years off, they would soon be spending more time together at home than they had in years. The prospect worried them. What would they talk about? This couple had never lost admiration and respect for each other, yet privately each of them had seriously considered separating for a long time.

When close friends announced their divorce after decades of marriage, Marge and Fred seemed to wake up. Was it too late for them, too, or was there some way for them to reengage with each other? To try, they traveled to Costa Rica, a place they had always wanted to visit. Late one night, the two of them went down to the beach in Tortuguero National Park. There they awaited the giant leatherback turtles, which would soon come in from the sea to lay their eggs under a nearly full moon. A naturalist had guided them down there, and Fred spoke with him quietly about the range of these turtles — as far north as Alaska and as far south as the Cape of Good Hope in Africa. Marge listened, impressed. She hadn't heard her husband talk about anything of substance for a long time.

Then, suddenly, there they were, the enormous, primordial turtles, emerging from the sea. Marge and Fred watched in wonder as the leatherbacks dug themselves into the sand to build nests and lay their eggs. Both were deeply moved.

The following morning, the couple enjoyed the liveliest conversation they'd had in years. The spark between Marge and Fred was the one they'd struck from the very beginning — a shared goal and the challenges they must meet to achieve it. Their conversation became stimulating, even exciting, as they began to envision how they could use their mutual skills to help the turtles. Their joint love of Central America and the outdoors, as well as their deep respect for animals and the wild, came together and spurred them to make a plan.

Soon after Marge and Fred returned from this trip, they developed a research project to determine how to save the sea turtle eggs from predators. Although their sex life never picked up, they regained a quiet joy in their marriage, founded on the pursuit of a shared vision.

Eventually, of course, their research came to an end — and their interests once again began to diverge. But that trip to Costa Rica, and its aftermath, taught Marge and Fred a leading principle about relationship: find a way to keep it vital. These days Marge and Fred make it a point to turn back to each other, from time to time, and collaborate on some overlapping interest. They also share important qualities — personal stability and kindness — which they have brought to the relationship from the start. These qualities have helped them find a careful, caring balance that serves both their separate and joint interests. When I last checked in with them, Marge and Fred were no longer frightened of retirement.

Some degree of parallel living takes place in most marriages. Actually, a little distance is a useful and healthy thing. The time we spend apart within a marriage allows us not only to grow as individuals but also to resolve some of our discontent with unmet expectations.

We can also ratchet up our satisfaction level simply by doing the things we enjoy, even if our partner doesn't join us. Say you like to bike on trails in the woods, and he doesn't. Why not find a local group and head out for a ride every Saturday morning? Possibilities for connection are out there, everywhere. The bottom line: if you choose to be in a marriage of independent souls, allow yourself to be surprised. With a bit of creativity and sufficient good will, your relationship may change unexpectedly in positive, loving ways.

Build a New Relationship

The final option of stage four is to build a new partnership. You'll notice that I include no option here to fix what's broken. Although I've characterized this stage as a crossroads, one path is closed to us — the way back. We can't regain what we've lost. We can, however, make good on old possibilities, and create new ones.

Master therapist Hedy Schleifer once remarked that she's had fourteen husbands in forty-plus years.[8] She didn't trade partners but continued to change her relationship with her husband. While this idea may not appeal to you at the moment, bear in mind that what appears to be a dead end may actually lead to all sorts of new destinations.

I worry about couples who characterize their decision to build a new foundation as an effort to "save the marriage." This intention often leads people away from any kind of reckoning that is deep, honest, and shared. Intent on reconciliation, partners fail to tell each other the truth because one fears the other will be disappointed or get angry again. They pretend to feel and think things that aren't true, and they land in a whole new mess.

The good news is that we can learn a lot during this fourth stage as long as we face our partners and ourselves square on. What we learn will indeed set us free — whether we stay or go it alone. We need to commit to some hard work at this point, however. First, we need to adopt a new approach to relationship and understand its components: (1) fair rules of conflict, (2) practices that build good will, (3) skills that improve communication, and (4) an understanding of the extraordinary new research on what makes a relationship healthy.

Second, we must journey into ourselves. We must look at our patterns — both those that protect us and those that connect us — as part of the dynamic of partnership. We need to explore our personal history, especially the influences of our family on our emotional development and current behavior.

Third, we must journey into the relationship — its past, present, and potential. How did it begin, what did it promise, and what are its strong points, as well as its weak ones? We must examine the dynamics and zero in on the behaviors that repeatedly lead to conflict and compromise our partnership. We must admit that some of the stories we tell — about ourselves and about our partner — may not contain the whole truth.

Time Out

A carefully planned separation — a sabbatical, so to speak — can be a step toward clarity. Ideally, this type of separation should be done with structure, clear expectations, goodwill, and the help of a third person. Some excellent books outline the promise and possibilities of such a strategy.[9]

Even when it's not carefully planned, however, time apart can lead to renewal. Once, following a talk on Love Cycles I gave at Rancho La Puerta in Tecate, Mexico, a tall, sixtyish woman with a head of beautiful silver hair approached me.

"Never marry a man you haven't already divorced," she said, and I asked her to tell me her story as we walked to the lounge for some peppermint tea.

Nan told me that she'd been married to Robert for twenty-five years. "Life was fine, he was fine, our relationship was fine, and I was bored to death with all the fineness," she told me. Just when life had never felt duller, she took on a new client, a talented writer several years her junior. As his literary agent, Nan met with him to discuss his career. They spoke for hours over lunch and coffee, first about his upcoming book tour, then about contemporary novels and poetry, and eventually about her personal passion, equestrian statues. Chip was the first person Nan had ever met who loved horse sculptures almost as much as she did. They showed each other their private collections and then began to visit local galleries and museums together regularly to see more.

They became lovers. Nan couldn't remember ever feeling so alive and connected. She and Chip spoke the same language, one that only they understood. Their lovemaking was passionate, thrilling. This affair, she convinced herself, couldn't hurt her marriage. On the contrary, she believed that her love affair only intensified her allegiance to, and affection for, Robert.

Nan lived in both relationships for several months. Then Robert walked into a restaurant one day and caught sight of her and Chip. He sensed immediately that they were intimate. Furious, he insisted that Nan cut off the affair. Although torn and guilty, she couldn't bring herself to do that. For years, she had yearned to love like this. How lucky she was to have found Chip! She couldn't let him go. Instead, she left her marriage.

Robert accepted her decision. To the amazement of their children and the disgust of his friends, he defended Nan's right to leave and was determined to divide their property and assets fairly. Given his misery, however, he avoided Nan as much as possible. Still, whenever they did happen to meet, Robert was unfailingly kind. Were you to ask him, he would tell you that he felt the better for the generous way in which he had treated her.

Nan was impressed by her ex-husband's courage and determination to remain wholehearted. Her new lover's behavior began to impress her less. Chip even made fun of Robert's fairness.

"He's kind of an Eagle Scout, isn't he," he sneered, after Nan said something nice about Robert's generosity. "I think he's trying to win you back. My niece would call that 'sucky' behavior. I can see why you got sick of him!"

This unkind streak was just one of several troubling qualities that Nan began to notice. Of course, all the things that had first attracted her to Chip remained true: he was creative, expressive, and held passionate and often original views on most subjects. Plus, there was their shared love of art.

Still, Chip pushed for what he wanted from her (and from just about everyone else, she noticed). When things didn't go his way, he sulked. He had no interest in her children, seldom asked her anything about her life, and found her dog annoying. His love notes dwindled, and so did his spontaneous gifts of books and chocolate.

Nan began to spend time with Robert again. At first they met for coffee to talk about family and the business in which they each still owned shares. Coffee led to pleasant walks and dinners. As she spent more time with him, Nan was reminded of some of Robert's other fine qualities: his quick humor and deep integrity, in addition to his fair-minded generosity.

"You've picked up color," she told him, by which she meant the vibrant new life he had built for himself without her. She began to realize that Chip was a self-centered adolescent compared to her mature, conscientious ex-husband.

Though she was astonished to realize it, she longed to renew her life with Robert. This feeling grew into a certainty: she had made a terrible mistake, and she let Robert know.

Robert was gentle but slow to reciprocate. He needed time to be sure that reconciliation was right for him. Eventually, he was receptive. Even then, however, he insisted that he and Nan live apart for several more months to take stock of all that had happened. Once upon a time, Robert's caution would have irked Nan. Now she respected his wisdom. His prudence no longer looked stodgy but attractive, even sexy. He was his own man, true to his values, even under great pressure.

By the time that Nan told me her story, she and Robert had been reunited for nine years.

Nan's husband had displayed the kind of *virtus ardens* — Latin for "courage under fire" — that many of us would hope to display under similar circumstances. It's easy to talk about "doing the hard work" of controlling our impulse to retaliate when we've been wounded. When we're actually cornered or betrayed, however, it's a whole other business to pull it off. It's good to remind ourselves that we can always choose to stretch into our higher selves, not necessarily to preserve our marriage, but to grow up ourselves. This decision to grow is the most critical one of all.

In the next chapter, we will drop in on Charlie and Megan again and see how such a decision can play out — even when surviving together seems all but impossible.

Chapter Seven

COUPLE ON THE EDGE

Even good marriages have recurring seasons,
and there can be some hard winters.
— LINDA AND CHARLIE BLOOM,
101 Things I Wish I Knew When I Got Married

Some couples can't seem to avoid a collision course. At the end of chapter 4, Charlie had just driven home early from a hunting trip and had stopped on the way to buy some of Megan's favorite flowers as a peace offering. He'd arrived home to an empty house and decided to take a vase of the irises upstairs, where Megan would encounter them as a pleasant surprise in their bedroom. There he'd found a copy of an email, which lay on her desk. The brief message, signed by someone named James, read like a love note.

Charlie felt like he'd been kicked in the solar plexus. He had collapsed onto the bed and curled into a ball. Don't make so much of it, he told himself. It might not mean anything; Megan would never stoop so low. But he remained coiled on the bed, unable to move.

A half hour later, he heard his wife and children come into the house. The dog barked. He took a deep breath, forced himself out of bed, and headed downstairs. There in the foyer stood Megan, dressed in white, her black hair arranged in that perfectly angled bob of hers.

At the sight of him, she arched an eyebrow. "You're back early."

"Yes." Then he smiled. For once, Charlie noticed how odd it was to smile at a time like this. Yet he did it all the time. *My camouflage*, he thought.

Megan planted a cool kiss on his cheek and began to talk about the dog's accident. He asked for details. She spotted the Siberian irises in the living room and thanked him. He hugged his kids and asked them about their plans for the afternoon. All the while he felt disembodied, as if the real Charlie were floating somewhere up on the ceiling, where he watched the robot Charlie go through the motions. He couldn't bring himself to mention the note from James.

The week unfolded as usual, at least on the surface. All so civilized. All so surreal. Then Megan asked Charlie to pick up some fresh spinach on the way home from the hospital, and he came home that evening empty-handed. "Whoops, sorry," he said, as he entered the kitchen and saw tomato wedges set out on a cutting board. "I completely forgot."

"You'd think you could remember to do one thing for me," she said, haughty and put-upon.

It was typical of Megan to strike that tone when she was annoyed. Usually, he could shrug it off. Now it infuriated him.

"You always find a way to let me know I'm not as perfect as you are," he exploded. "You complain about my clothes, what I read, even the way I like to unwind. This is just one more crime, forgetting to go to the store after putting in a sixty-hour week." He paused, willing himself to calm down. Megan ignored him, as was her way, turning to more important matters such as cutting the ends off the asparagus.

Later that night, as they watched a TV program in the family room, he said to her, quietly, "We're pretty disillusioned with each other; let's face it."

"Yeah, let's," she snapped.

Charlie felt the rage rising again. "Maybe you're not quite as perfect as you pretend to be?"

"Aside from wanting to pick a fight, whatever are you talking about? Perfect or not, I do manage most of what it takes to run this household," Megan said coolly, "which you seem more than happy to leave to me."

"And do you manage James as well?"

Megan stared at him, openmouthed.

Charlie was surprised by the pleasure he felt at catching her out. It was his moment of righteous indignation. A few more moments passed before he could control himself enough to speak again. "You forgot something yourself," he told her, as calmly as he could, and "it's probably a bigger deal than spinach. You left a copy of an email from him, out there on the desk."

He could hear her quick intake of breath. When he turned to look at her, though, she wouldn't meet his gaze. When she finally spoke, she had regained some semblance of cool.

"Okay. So now you know."

"Exactly what is it that I know?"

This time she did look him in the eyes. "You read the message."

"Let's cut to the chase. Are you having an affair?"

She went silent again. Deliberating, it seemed, choosing her words. "Yes," she said, at last. "I think I really am in love with him. So, yes, you could say I'm having an affair."

She had met James at the tennis club. He was the divorced father of one of their son's best friends.

"How could you?" he hissed. To hear his wife admit to cheating on him — with someone connected to their young son, no less — filled him with hatred and disgust. He stormed out of the room, unsure which one of them he wanted to hurt more, Megan or James. The intensity of his feelings scared him. One thing he knew for certain: he wasn't fit company for his children. He went upstairs, packed a suitcase, scribbled a note as to his general whereabouts, and headed out to a hotel.

A War of Desperation

Over the next two days, the infuriated husband and the rational man waged war in Charlie's head. For the first time in his career, he called in sick to his office. He didn't sleep. He barely ate. He paced the floor of the hotel room and let his imagination torture him with the details of his wife's affair. He considered how he would confront James. He would serve Megan with divorce papers, and again he felt pleasure that his absolute contempt might hurt her.

The rational side of Charlie's brain, meanwhile, warned him away from vengeance. Retaliation would only deepen the disaster. He didn't want to behave in a way that would hurt their children. They were already hurt; he didn't want this nightmare to be any grimmer for them than it had to be.

Still, his inner storm raged. He'd worked so hard to make theirs a happy life! But Megan had taken the joy out of everything. Without warning, Charlie's fury gave way to heartbreak. He threw himself on the bed and wept into his pillow. At this release of emotions, he relaxed enough to feel the full extent of his exhaustion. He slept.

When he awoke the next morning, he missed his kids, instantly and painfully. For their sake, at least, he needed to begin some kind of conversation with Megan. When he called her, she suggested they find a third person, a therapist, to meet with. In his pediatric practice, Charlie had never hesitated to recommend psychotherapy when he saw signs of psychological distress in his young patients. For himself, however, counseling had always seemed out of the question. Where he came from, people sorted out their personal problems themselves. You do what needs to be done, and you don't blubber about it. Now, though, he felt desperate and confused. He agreed to see a marriage counselor.

A day or two later, when he had gone back to work, his cell phone rang. "Uh, hi," a familiar voice said. "It's me. I want to try and work this out with you, Charlie. I really do."

"I don't know if we can, Megan," he replied. He hesitated for a moment. "But I'm willing to try."

Courage

The next afternoon, the couple walked into my office for the first time. I asked why they had come and what they wanted to accomplish.

"I want to save the marriage," Megan began, "but I don't know how."

"This mess is not what I signed up for," Charlie said. "I want to go back to how it was in the beginning, when we loved being us."

What I said then surprised them both. "Let's start by acknowledging that the marriage is over. It's time to let it go."

"What? But that's not what we came here to do," Megan said, her voice full of alarm.

"Yeah, I'm not saying that I want to let this go," Charlie chimed in. "You're moving way too fast here."

"I understand," I nodded. "What I'm asking you to do is to acknowledge that the marriage you had — the old one — is done," I said. "Perhaps it's possible to create a new marriage. That's something you'll discover as we work together."

Over the next several months, the three of us met weekly. Charlie and Megan often felt anxious, not knowing where they were headed, but they committed themselves to working on the relationship. Megan cut off all contact with James and answered all Charlie's questions about the relationship, no matter how painful the conversation became. To her credit, she did not try to blame Charlie in any way; she took total responsibility for her choice to cross the line into an affair. Both of them began to understand that there was no going back to what once was. We had two issues to manage in our work together: Megan's affair, for which she was responsible, and the difficulties in the marriage, for which both were culpable. I encouraged them to explore their own part in the estrangement and to understand how it had occurred. Gradually, both began to focus on where they were in their lives and how they had gotten there.

Delving Deep

Megan had always been interested in psychology. Fairly early in the therapeutic process, she became intrigued by the idea that both she and Charlie had contributed to the problems between them. She was game for delving into her psyche and trying to make sense of what she found there.

"I know why I just closed down," she said, midway through one of our sessions. "Charlie can be just like my mother in the oddest ways. Sometimes I feel just like I did as a child — only seen for what I do, not for who I am."

She had fallen in love with the cute farm boy who had become the kids' doctor everyone loved. Megan might appear cool and controlled, but she actually longed for intimate conversation and emotional connection. Charlie's easygoing style and warmth appealed to her, she said, because "I wanted to melt. I hoped Charlie could help me do that — in a safe and loving place."

What Megan hadn't counted on was how emotionally unavailable Charlie would prove to be. Except during the first stage of their love, when he seemed to want to share his very soul with her, Charlie seemed little interested in what Megan thought of as "deep conversation" that involved sharing feelings, aspirations, and doubts. The frenetic socializing they'd long shared had slowed down to the point where his idea of satisfying connection was to have a few beers with his friends and watch a basketball game.

She knew that her husband was tired when came home from the hospital. But did he really have to eat dinner in near-silence and fall asleep shortly after the children's bedtime? Frustration, Megan admitted, had made her grimmer and more sarcastic with him than she wanted to be. When he brushed her off in ways she found punishing, she retaliated by needling and chiding.

Over the past few years, their sex life had dropped off precipitously. Charlie claimed exhaustion, and she didn't pressure him, because she never felt that he was making love to her, Megan. "I don't feel like you see me — or know me," she told him.

It was the same feeling she'd had growing up. As the only child of two highly successful people, Megan had felt like a trophy kid. Her parents were proud of her achievements — her perfect grades, her skill in sports, her talent in music and dance, and her good looks. But they never asked her how she felt or what she thought.

Megan knew she was out of line when she took up with James, but out of line was exactly where she wanted to be. Here was someone who seemed to delight in her for being the girl she'd never been allowed to be — someone who just wanted to kick back and enjoy herself. He took the initiative to make fun things happen. He surprised her with tickets to the opera and no-special-reason picnics; once he reserved a room at the most luxurious hotel in town, where champagne arrived on a silver tray.

With James, she didn't have to be the responsible adult or the accomplished professional or the model mom. She didn't have to be so damned nice all the time, either. She and James loved to mimic people. No harm done, they said to each other; ridicule was just a way to blow off steam. No need to be serious, to be in charge, to be impeccable in dress and decorum. No need to be perfect.

Still, the depth of despair she had felt the night Charlie left was horrendous. As she lay in bed alone, Megan realized that even though Charlie drove her crazy, she wanted to stay married to him. She admired so much about him, and she didn't want to put the kids through a divorce. Although the prospect of losing James was painful, she remained true to her promise not to see him again and continued to answer Charlie's questions about their clandestine relationship with courageous honesty.

Charlie Remembers

As my weekly sessions with the couple continued, it became clear that Charlie didn't share Megan's enthusiasm for "psychological sleuthing," as he put it. "These constant referrals to our childhoods are getting annoying," he said one afternoon. "I think we need to look at what's happening right now."

For Charlie, the immediate issue was trust — or, more accurately, the lack of it. Megan's fling with James was the elephant in the room, of course, and the elephant was still lumbering about. She insisted that she'd stopped seeing James, but Charlie didn't believe her. "I can't stop thinking about it," he admitted. "I go over it in my mind. I don't know if I can ever trust her again. As for forgiveness?" He shook his head. "It doesn't come easy to me."

To nearly everyone who knew him, Charlie was a "nice guy." Only, this assessment wasn't the whole truth. As we worked together, he began to see that he needed to connect with his darker feelings — especially anger. His avoidance of conflict had made him one-dimensional. "Easygoing Charlie" had always left it to Megan to be the "angry one."

In their sessions with me, the couple gradually reversed their customary roles. Charlie became the critical one.

"Wow. You never stop with your superiority, do you?" he said to Megan one day. Disgust dripped from his voice. "You name-drop constantly. It's embarrassing when you think you need to tell our babysitter where you went to school."

It was clear to me that the anger that lay buried in Charlie was surfacing, and also that he would need to learn how to express it in ways that his wife could hear — and bear.

One evening, he came into our session and just opened up. "I was thinking of Megan's betrayal again. I was all torn up, as usual. Then it hit me how my mom had done that."

He sighed heavily. "My dad cheated on her, and she punished him for the next forty years. I know what that did to my brothers and me. Do I want to do that to my own family?"

Megan looked taken aback. "I didn't know that about your parents."

"Nobody does. I've never talked about it."

Megan and I listened as he told the story for the first time. It all started back in the hotel room, where he'd fled right after he'd found out about James. Just as he'd begun to drift off into much-needed sleep, old memories began to surface. They were ones he'd buried a long time ago.

Six-year-old Charlie awoke to the sound of his parents' voices, raised in argument downstairs. He got out of bed and tiptoed to the edge of the stairs in his gunslinger pajamas. His father, usually loud and demanding, was speaking in a low voice while his mother, whom most people considered a saint, was alternately crying and yelling, "How could you do this to our family?"

His father's words were so soft that Charlie couldn't make all of them out. But the sorrow and anger he did hear filled the little boy with fear and distress as he crept back to bed. As Charlie related the story, he looked small and stricken. It was as though he'd traveled back in time to reinhabit that miserable little boy.

The next morning, his parents behaved as though nothing had happened. But things did change in his family, and quickly. Within a couple of days after the argument, a deliveryman came to the house and replaced his parent's double bed with twin beds. Two weeks later, the family changed churches with no explanation. His father ceased his high-handed treatment of his wife and turned his dissatisfaction on his children, especially Charlie, the eldest. But in fact, Charlie seldom saw his dad anymore. From dawn to dark, his dad did chores out on the farm. "My family used to have a lot of fun together," he said. "Now there was just this heavy silence all the time."

As a child, Charlie had no choice but to live with parents who remained side by side but estranged ever after. He'd tried hard to make sense of the disintegration. A silent war had begun during that argument he overheard, yet no one ever acknowledged it had happened. The puzzlement and the pain were his to sort out alone.

He finally decided that it was farm life, with all its hard work, that had estranged his parents from each other. It was an existence of never-ending uncertainty and backbreaking labor. He wouldn't make the same mistake; he would leave the land. Get as far away from it all as he could. "And that pretty much set me on my life course," he told us, his voice shaky. "I went to college, applied to med school. I made sure I'd never, ever be my parents."

When I looked over at Megan, I saw that her features had softened. She was obviously touched by her husband's story and his display of vulnerability. She seemed to have forgotten herself and her complaints. She leaned over toward him, gently pressing her hand on his. "I'm sorry," she whispered.

During our next meeting, Megan pulled out a couple of photograph albums — one of photos taken of her as a child and the other of Charlie growing up with his family. The couple pulled their chairs close together and pored over the pictures for a few minutes. Their heads practically touched, and when they looked up at me, their faces were filled with affection.

Megan removed two of the photographs from the albums, one of each of them as children, and handed them to me.

"You're both recognizable," I said with a smile as I looked at the children they used to be. There was Charlie, minus two front teeth, laughing intensely at something his brother was saying. There was Megan, holding a cat on her lap, with a carefree look on her face that I'd seen only in flashes.

"What made you want to bring these photos in today, Megan?" I asked.

"I don't know," she began, seeming to search for words. "There's something so endearing in these children; they remind me of who we once were. I can see the same kind of sweetness in our own kids." Her voice was wistful.

For a moment, Charlie and I just sat there and took in Megan's words. I had never seen her look so tender.

The Best Medicine

As they learned more about themselves and each other, this couple gradually began to reach out to each other. Charlie and Megan had the right instincts. They understood that the breakdown in their marriage could put them on the path to renewal. The bigger challenge was for them to understand the different ways in which they each blocked the intimacy they claimed they wanted.

I knew they had turned a corner when I saw how quick they were to realize their stumbles into old, troubled patterns and how quick they were to pull themselves out again, often with a laugh about their slipups. There were some bold moves, too. Charlie went out and bought a funny tie and wore it to a party with Megan. I noticed how relaxed they both seemed as they told me about the choice of the tie and the effects it had on them both. For Charlie, it was liberating, a chance to express his zany sense of humor.

With a genuine smile, Megan described herself as "cautiously amused" and reported how their friends seemed to enjoy her husband when he clowned around. I had the sense she was finally beginning to enjoy this side of her husband, too.

In one of our last sessions together, Megan handed Charlie a magazine, opened to a particular page, and pointed to a sentence she had underlined. It was one that the actress Joanne Woodward had written about her late husband, Paul Newman. Charlie read it aloud, "Sexiness wears thin after a while and beauty fades, but to be married to a man who makes you laugh every day, ah, now that is a treat."

Charlie looked across at his wife and smiled. This time, it was no camouflage; it was a real smile.

This couple will remain imperfect, of course, no matter how much work they do to heal and grow. They won't always be able to give and receive unconditionally. Nor will they always please each other in every way. Each, however, is on the road to achieving something vital — self-actualization. Megan was unflinching in her willingness to take responsibility for the affair and not blame Charlie in any way. Charlie was able to recognize that the challenges of forgiving such a betrayal — a massive undertaking for anyone — was compounded by his tendency to hold secret grudges and use them as fuel for indignation and a sense of superiority. Each partner found a way to face and accept the many disappointments of their relationship and to manage their own troubling thoughts and reactions. It is through such work over a lifetime that each of us can reach our highest, healthiest potential — both as an individual and as part of a couple. We can begin to open our hearts.

Chapter Eight

OUR SEXUAL CYCLES

The secret of sex is that…there is no secret.
Be generous. Be kind. Make love first, then have sex.

— SAM KEEN, in conversation with the author

The benefits of an active sex life are well known. Research has demonstrated that sex relieves stress, improves sleep, lowers blood pressure, improves heart health, and even boosts immunity so that we're less susceptible to colds and infections. Regular lovemaking boosts self-esteem, reduces depression, and reportedly reduces the risk of prostate cancer. The increased oxytocin and endorphins released during sex reduce pain while they expand generosity, openhearted feelings, and the possibility of greater emotional intimacy between partners.[1]

Despite all the evidence showing that sex is good for us, psychologists and therapists such as Barry McCarthy at American University in Washington, DC, estimate that one in five couples have given up on sex permanently.[2] The reasons are myriad: unresolved power struggles; complications from unhealed betrayals; kids, who may sleep between you in bed or leave you exhausted because you get up in the middle of the night to care for them; normal drops in testosterone over time; and just about anything that makes you feel bad physically, from sleep disorders and depression to poor fitness and knee pain.

And let's not forget the difference in the level of desire, one of the major complaints couples have. There's a famous scene in the Woody Allen movie *Annie Hall* in which Alvy Singer and Annie appear in split-screen images. Each is speaking to his or her own therapist.

Alvy's therapist asks, "How often do you sleep together?"

Alvy laments, "Hardly ever, maybe three times a week."

Annie's therapist inquires, "Do you have sex often?"

"Constantly," says Annie, annoyed. "I'd say three times a week."[3]

Each of them is telling the truth through the filter of their own felt experience. Yet it isn't necessarily the difference in sex drive that causes the frustration. Sometimes it's the conviction that our partner's level of desire is a direct reflection of her feelings for us, or that our being different sexually from our partner somehow makes us wrong. This issue can cause trouble during any stage of love except the first one, when most of us feel like we can't get enough of our luscious hunk (or babe) of a partner.

In *Annie Hall*, Alvy interprets Annie's relatively low interest in sex as a sign that she doesn't really love him, that she's cold-hearted. Annie may assume that Alvy doesn't love her either, that he's only interested in satisfying his insatiable lust. What's more likely, however, is that our sexual proclivities are a direct reflection of our hormonal levels rather than a measure of how much we love our partner.

When it comes to sex, some of us are light switches, always ready to be turned on. Others are like slow-warming irons, or even irons that barely heat up at all. All these hormonal levels are normal, and it's also normal for them to change throughout our lives.

Yet it's just as normal for us to take our partner's level of desire personally. If you're the one with the lower sexual desire, you may feel inadequate on the one hand and bullied on the other. If you're highly charged, you may feel uncherished by a partner who controls the quantity of your sex life through intermittent availability.

Scenes from a Marriage

On the way home from a party, Julie complained to her husband, Roger: "You flirted with every good-looking woman in the room. It made me feel like I'm not enough for you."

Roger is a classic high-testosterone male. A former professional athlete, he's now a manager in the highly competitive pharmaceutical sales industry. Although he thinks about sex all the time and notices women constantly, his wide-ranging sexual radar has little to do with how attractive he finds Julie. He finds her delicious, actually. He's never had sex outside his marriage. His focus on sex is just part of how he's made.

Julie herself feels very little desire these days. That wasn't always the case. The couple's first stage of love, when she'd experienced the Merge with Roger, lasted three years. Although most of her fantasies during those years centered on the romantic aspects of the relationship rather than on the sexual ones, Julie was happily turned on by the chemical love potion released in the first stage. In fact, she was amazed at the change in herself — how sexy she felt and how often she thought about "doing it." Roger, meanwhile, was delighted that "he" could turn her on so much.

Once they entered the second stage of their relationship, Doubt and Denial, Julie found Roger's constant need for sex tiresome. She hid her lack of enthusiasm because she was still "so in love with him." When their son, Austin, was born, however, her desire plummeted to the basement. She felt relief: the baby gave her a good excuse to be less sexually available. But she also felt afraid that her flagging libido was a sign that she was falling out of love with her husband.

Not so: Julie's drop in desire was simply a sign that her body had returned to its normal state of relatively low sexual desire after the love potion of the first stage had worn off. Her desire was then lowered further by the presence in her bloodstream of a new love chemical, namely oxytocin, which had kicked in after Austin was born. This "cuddle chemical" certainly increased her feelings of warmth and affection, but they were directed mostly toward her new baby, which, from Roger's perspective, made her appear even more unavailable.

Although Roger felt concern and even resentment when Julie turned away from him in bed, he told himself things would "get back to normal" once the baby grew more independent. Birth and motherhood do affect sex drive, so Roger's assessment was correct, except for one crucial element. The "normal" he recalled from their early sex life actually *wasn't* normal for Julie, whose typically low desire was only temporarily heightened during the first stage of their relationship.[4]

As their baby grew, so did their disagreements. Roger and Julie got caught in infinity loops: their conflicts moved in circles and never got resolved. Julie was "overly protective" of Austin; Roger was "careless" and took too many risks with him. Roger wanted to save money and complained that Julie spent too much.

Julie felt stung and hurt. He must value his family very little, she thought, to want to spend so little on her and Austin.

By the time this couple entered the third stage of love, they were plenty disillusioned. They suffered from lumpy-carpet syndrome as well, given that they were forever trying to hide the unmet needs that lay beneath their grievances. As they stood in their kitchen one day, those needs began to spill out.

Julie was making a fresh vegetable salad when Roger came up behind her and put his arms around her. She stiffened. He dropped his arms. He was tired of Julie's rejections. Because he didn't know how else to manage the hurt, he got angry.

"All I did was put my arms around you," Roger snapped. "And you froze me out — again."

"You haven't bothered to have a conversation with me in months," Julie countered. "And then you come on to me when I'm trying to make dinner."

"I wasn't coming on to you," Roger said. "Believe me, I don't try that anymore. We haven't made love in months."

"Well, how can I want to, when you don't even ask me how my day went?" Julie spun around and faced him, her face tight with anger. "You're too busy for me. But not for sex."

"Maybe if we had sex," Roger retorted, "we'd have a relationship." He sighed loudly and walked away.

I wish I'd known Roger was such a sex maniac before I married him, Julie thought, furiously slicing cucumbers.

I ought to see if I can find a good psychiatrist for her, Roger thought as he stalked out of the kitchen. *Julie needs some help for her frigidity.*

Here we have two normal human beings who have pathologized each other. Each feels isolated and sad. They move further apart and no longer touch each other. Each believes the problem is that there is something wrong with the other.

In the third stage, disconnections grow more challenging, and ruptures can be dramatic. A partner with a low sex drive may refuse sex altogether, and the discrepancy in desire becomes stark. Once positive emotional contact flags, it's harder to negotiate differences. Ironically, this is when we need connection most.

One of the most important things for couples to understand is that our sex lives don't need to be determined by our levels of desire. A person who thinks about sex all the time needn't suffer or feel isolated. Even if your partner seldom thinks of sex, he or she can still be aroused. The solution is to manage the differences, not to personalize them. And the secret is to keep as much goodwill as possible between you, so that this difference doesn't become the source of a power struggle.

For example, a massage from Roger might get Julie turned on, even if she doesn't feel desire when he starts. When they're making love, she might even think, *Hey, this is great! Why don't we do it more?*

Roger, meanwhile, may realize that Julie's lack of interest isn't an absence of love. Perhaps they can negotiate lovemaking sessions that are just for him and others that are just for her. (For example, sometimes Julie can have a foot or body massage with no other expectations.) If enough good connection begins to happen between them, they might even be able to laugh about the discrepancy in their levels of desire and be glad that so much else does work well.

Sex and State of Mind

What could hinder this couple from the enjoyment of good-enough sex, however, is a sense of inadequacy, which many of us feel with respect to the cultural standards that apply to sexuality.

Most people define a good sex life on the basis of their memories of early romantic love, blended with all the hot sex they've seen on TV and movie screens, topped off with all the steamy scenes they've read about, whether in great literature or in soft porn. We also compare our normal, imperfect bodies — our partner's and our own — with those of the perfect models we see in advertisements. (And aging couples, take note: nowhere are these models more beautiful than in TV ads for Viagra!)

Let's look a little more closely at these sexual standards, for they affect nearly everyone, women and men alike. In our aggressively youth-centered culture, concepts of what constitutes a good sex life tend to be based on what might work for a twenty-five-year-old in the throes of first-stage love — on a very good day. As we age, it's easy to feel discouraged by these unrealistic performance standards. Everywhere we turn, our culture encourages us to believe that healthy sexuality means that we:

- possess a sex drive that is both high and equal to that of our partner;
- enjoy not one orgasm but several, all of them synchronized with those of our partner; and
- can read our partner's mind perfectly and are therefore able to please him or her without asking or experimenting with the possibilities first.

If we accept these wildly unrealistic expectations as the norm, it's all but impossible to feel sexually vital. Having sex that is merely good enough sounds like getting a C on a report card. We don't make the grade, and we feel bad about ourselves. In fact, I believe that a sense of inadequacy underlies nearly all the sexual problems that couples encounter. Our biggest and toughest sexual challenge may not be to solve this or that particular bedroom issue but rather to learn how to accept and embrace our precious human selves, just as we are.

So how do we resist the constant messages our culture sends us — to be very young, very fit, and very beautiful — and instead accept ourselves as we are with every right to fully enjoy our sexual selves? The key is not to amass tools for a ramped-up sex life but to encourage a gentle, inner shift. If we can come to a generous acceptance of our own human limitations, we can begin to find our way back to our partner. A more relaxed standard allows us to forget all the hype and just let ourselves feel just how good good-enough sex can be. Now the door is open for something new to happen.

Something New

Most of us want something new to happen. The known and predictable can be deadening. Thirty years of the same old person with the same, annoying ways of combing his hair, holding his coffee cup, or telling a story can be a real turnoff. Let's not even get started talking about nasty noises and flossing. And yet when we see that same old person in a new way, we notice all kinds of surprising and attractive turn-ons.

One night, about fifteen years into my marriage, my husband and I were at a wedding. Tim asked me to dance, but the floor was full of younger people, my feet were already sore, and I was engaged in lively conversation with several of our friends. I said, "No thanks." A few minutes later, a beautiful young woman tapped my husband's arm and invited him out on to the dance floor. He went happily.

Suddenly I saw him in a totally different light. As he moved to the wild music, laughing with this other woman, he seemed more attractive than he had in ages. For a little while I just watched, feeling a mixture of irritation and interest. Then I walked over and cut in on the other woman. My husband and I stayed at the party for another hour, dancing and laughing, and the evening turned out to be memorable for all the flirtatious fun between us. The soreness in my feet disappeared entirely.

In one of my supervision groups, a therapist described her work with a couple who had decided to divorce. Shortly after they made the decision, they had the biggest fight of their marriage. Thoroughly fed up with each other, they felt free at last to dispense with any effort to keep the relationship "happy and nice" and free to say things that had gone unsaid for years. She complained about all the weight he'd gained. He carped about how much money she spent on frivolous things. She admitted she couldn't stand his mother. He condemned her for overzealous care of dogs and neglect of people. They then proceeded to have the most passionate sex they'd ever known.

All the other therapists laughed; it was a familiar story.

It's true that an argument can heighten desire. Sometimes when we're about to cut loose, we let loose. We say all the things we've held in check for years. We surprise our partners and ourselves. The lumpy carpet gets flattened out, and we can feel surprisingly disarmed, and closer.

Jealousy can rekindle romantic interest, and a big fight can be erotic. Yet I don't recommend the pursuit of either jealousy or anger as a strategy: both emotions are risky. They can create distance and lead to alienation rather than to good sex. But they do point to a paradox: the comfortable predictability of ordinary life can prevent us from experiencing our partner in a new way, a way that may be exciting and erotic.

Conventional psychological wisdom has it that we must first resolve our power struggles and reconnect emotionally before we can rebuild our sex lives on firm ground. Even when couples succeed and reconnect, however, not all of them rekindle sexually. Many couples who choose to stay in their relationship find that their sex drives don't automatically soar as their commitment deepens. The wild success of erotic fiction, the prevalence of extramarital affairs, and the perpetual lure of the forbidden tell us otherwise. It's quite possible that what most monogamous couples need to do instead is to find ways to fulfill the domestic need for the predictable while they indulge the erotic need for the new — but under the same roof with the same person. We want to minimize risk while maximizing passion.

In her groundbreaking book *Mating in Captivity*, Esther Perel says, "We want it all, and we want it with one person. Reconciling the domestic and the erotic is a delicate balancing act that we achieve intermittently at best."[5]

Sex and Aging

The normal aging process creates its own stresses. Menopause, ill health, and the side effects of medications can all take their toll on us sexually.[6]

Yet we may experience unexpected changes as well. Over time a woman with a low sex drive may find her mind filled with erotic fantasies. Mr. Light Switch may find that he's unable to keep an erection.

Unfortunately, some people respond to normal physiological changes as a signal that they've reached the end of their sex lives. They assume this just because at age forty they no longer feel like the "hottie" they were when they were twenty or thirty. Normal hormonal changes for males can be particularly difficult if they've been raised to believe that a readily erect penis is a fundamental marker of manhood.

In fact, I've long observed that men are as likely as women to put an end to the sex in their marriages. They conclude that something is wrong with them because they can no longer get an erection or because they can't hold it as long as they once could. I often tell clients that if on any given day you lined up every man who was shopping at Wal-Mart, catching a plane at O'Hare Airport, or watching a ball game on TV and got them to tell the truth about their sexuality, half of them would admit to having a problem. They would admit that their penis doesn't stand up when they want it to or for long enough, or that it does at the wrong times, or that they ejaculate too quickly, too slowly, or not at all.

None of these problems necessarily qualifies as a dysfunction. But because men almost never share these experiences with one another, they're left to compare themselves with the performance levels other men brag about or what they see on TV, in the movies, or on the Internet. Once again, they subscribe to standards that can prove hazardous to their well-being.

Sex at a Certain Age

I was about to finish a two-day session with Maggie and Art, clients of mine whom I traveled to New York City to work with. Our last session was to take place the following evening. Then Maggie called to say that Art, who was a specialty surgeon, had an emergency and couldn't make it. Could she bring her mother along instead?

Maggie described her mother as "pushing ninety and in perfect physical health," and went on to say, "Her mind is sharper than mine is. The problem, I think, is emotional." Maggie bit her lip. "My father died three years ago, and Mom has been losing weight ever since. She doesn't go anywhere. The assisted-living staff thinks she's terribly depressed, but nobody can find anything wrong with her. She's never seen a counselor, but I think I could get her to come see you."

That evening Maggie entered my hotel suite with her mother, Helen. For the most part, Maggie's mom matched my mental picture of a woman at age eighty-plus: her hair was short and blue tinged from an inexpensive rinse, and she wore an aqua-colored pantsuit with thick-soled shoes. Less expected was the rouge. A bright little circle was painted in the center of each cheek, despite a world map of wrinkles etched into her face.

"Ma, we're worried about you," Maggie began, after the two had settled into comfortable chairs across from me. "We want you to start living again and enjoy the time you have left with us."

Helen just looked at her hands. Large blue veins protruded from her skin. For thirty minutes, she sat silently and seemed to grow smaller, while her daughter's voice grew louder and faster as she listed her concerns.

This is going nowhere, I thought. Then, suddenly, I was gripped by an urge — and I went with it. "Helen," I asked, "would you like to talk with me alone for a few moments?"

She nodded.

Dutifully, Maggie went out for a cup of tea, giving us the last twenty minutes of the session to ourselves. As soon as she left, I leaned in toward Helen.

"I bet you miss him," I said softly.

Again, she nodded. For a few moments, we were silent. Then she began to weep, quietly and with a depth of sorrow that startled me. Through her tears, she spoke.

"I finally learned how to love him. It took nearly seventy years and lots of trouble, but we finally learned."

"You shared a whole lifetime," I said.

"Yes, but that wasn't it. We were married at seventeen, and a lot of those first decades together weren't so good."

Helen looked away. When she spoke again, she didn't meet my gaze. "A few years before he died, I looked at Sam one day and realized we were near the end of our lives.

" 'Sam,' I said, 'Let's bury all the hatchets. Let's use the time we have left to be kind to one another.'

"At first he looked annoyed, the same old tough Sam." Helen pursed her lips slightly. "But then he said, 'Helen, you're right.' And that shocked me. 'You're usually right,' he said. 'I've never told you some things I should've — that you make each day fresh, you never hold a grudge, and you've made me laugh all these years. I should appreciate you more.' "

Helen was stunned. Here was a man who rarely uttered more than four words at a time and always seemed so out of reach. But when he spoke to her like that, it was magic. She could see through his old age. And there he was, the ardent young man she'd met so many years ago. From then on, things began to change.

"We hadn't even hugged in years. But we had an awkward embrace and, well, other things happened, too. After a while nature took its course." Helen's words practically spilled out of her. Her face was lit with a new liveliness. "I miss lying next to him at night," she went on. "The smell of him. The feel of that sweet, bald head against my skin." She hesitated. "I miss our physical life," she finally said. "You know, our making love." I could hear the wistfulness in her voice.

Helen surprised me. I'd had no idea that women in their eighties and nineties had active sex lives, or that they could catch fire so late in life. Her story led me to look at the research available on sex and older women. The AARP surveyed more than eight hundred older women in Southern California, ages forty to a hundred, with results published in the *American Journal of Medicine* in 2012.[7] The survey found that women under the age of fifty-five and women older than eighty were the two groups most likely to say that their sexual satisfaction had increased with age, despite the fact that frequency of arousal and orgasm had decreased.

Sex therapist Wendy Maltz has written that, unlike other species, we humans possess a sexuality that can last decades beyond the years of fertility and procreation. In fact, barring serious health problems, we have the ability to stay sexually active (with or without a partner) until we die.[8]

Maltz recalls the words of Freda, an eighty-seven-year-old poet, who told her that she enjoys pleasuring herself to orgasm every day and imagining a man with a big erection wanting to make love to her. "You never lose your fancies," Freda chuckled.

Freda doesn't speak for everyone, of course, as research has shown. And, unfortunately, it's not just sex itself that's threatened by older people's tendency to dial down bodily expressions of connection. Some couples no longer touch each other at all, at least not deliberately. No longer do they offer up a massage for a tired back or aching feet, hug each other tight, or even hold hands. When we let these simple, human forms of connection diminish, we can end up feeling starved. In fact, we need the soothing comfort of physical reassurance more than ever as we grow older. Skin delights in being touched; bodies yearn to connect.

We have options and information available to us as never before to jump-start and maintain our sexuality in relationships at any age. Dr. Barry McCarthy, for example, has contributed a bedrock of information, skills, and tools to help anyone bring their sexual relationship back to life. "Sexuality energizes your bond and reinforces feelings of desire and desirability," he writes in a blog post on *Psychology Today*. "Paradoxically, dysfunctional, conflicting, or avoidant sexuality has an inordinately powerful role, draining intimacy and threatening relational stability."[9]

Sex and the Sensual

The sensual pleasures of our creature selves are available to all of us, throughout our lives. Sound: a chorus in song, the vibration of a cello string, or the unexpected voice of a loved one on the other end of the phone. Taste: fresh strawberries, brandy, chocolate. Touch: the solace of skin upon skin, the softness of a companion animal's fur, the warmth of sand on our bodies at the beach. Sight: a mountain vista, a dogwood in spring, a brilliant sunset. Smell: clean linen, honeysuckle, orchard peaches. Such sensual pleasures transcend age, era, culture, and gender. They're at the essence of being human. Novelist Edith Wharton evoked this sensual birthright in a brief passage from her 1920 classic, *The Age of Innocence*: " 'Then stay with me a little longer,' Madame Olenska said in a low tone, just touching his knee with her plumed fan. It was the lightest touch, but it thrilled him like a caress."[10]

Pleasure — the touch of feathers on a knee — allows us to feel fully alive. We don't need lessons or manuals to appreciate such moments. We just need to discover what keeps us at bay from our sensuality and sexuality. Maybe we need to move our child out of the bed between us. Or bury the hatchets before we're in our eighties, as Helen and Sam did. Or simply understand that we're made to touch, hold, and enjoy each other throughout our lives.

Remember that erotic images, sensual pleasures, and words from love poems speak to something deep within each of us, regardless of our age, health, or relationship status. We're almost never beyond the point when we can start again. This elemental truth comes alive in the final pages of James Joyce's *Ulysses*, when Molly Bloom engages in a reverie about herself and her husband of many years. After a ten-year winter of celibacy in her marriage, Molly remembers the early times with her husband,

the delicious Merge they once enjoyed, and she accepts her husband back into her bed: "And then I asked him with my eyes
to ask again yes and then he asked me would I yes to say yes
my mountain flower and first I put my arms around him yes and
drew him down to me so he could feel my breasts all perfume yes
and his heart was going like mad and yes I said yes I will Yes."[11]

Chapter Nine

THE FINE ART OF DIFFERENTIATION

Only through our connectedness to others can we really know
and enhance the self. And only through working on the self
can we begin to enhance our connectedness to others.

— HARRIET LERNER, *The Dance of Intimacy*

Most of us live with two competing urges — to merge
and to feel independent. If we can strike a balance between them,
however, we can reconcile these urges: we can connect deeply
with our partner and still feel whole, even when we're alone.

The more we feel a solid sense of self, the more we can accept
our partner's differences. We no longer ask in frustration, "Why
aren't you *me*?" At a deep level, we truly get that our partner is
a separate and whole individual, just as we are. This recognition
and acceptance of separateness is what it means to be differentiated. By helping us move skillfully and comfortably between
relationship and independence, between connection and solitude, differentiation is at the heart of a healthy self and a healthy
relationship.

Separate and Together

Martha's dog, Barney, was a pugnacious little pug, but she loved him dearly. Several years back, she'd brought him home from a rescue organization, and her affectionate, soothing manner had gradually calmed him — unless a man happened to walk through the door. Barney retained a special aversion to men, growling and snarling at all Martha's male friends, no matter how often they came to visit.

Some years later Martha met and married Mark, who, unfortunately, disliked dogs almost as much as Barney disliked men. At first it galled Mark to have to compete with a dog for Martha's affection. Martha traveled a lot in her line of legal work, which meant dog and man were left to fend for themselves for days at a time. In the evening, Mark would dread the return home to their apartment, empty of Martha but full of the sound and fury of Barney.

Yet it wasn't long before he and the pug learned to coexist. Mark overcame his first response of outrage to Barney's crazed barking and would say as gently as he could manage, "Barney, Barney, it's all okay." Barney certainly didn't wag his stumpy tail in response, but he did begin to settle down in Mark's presence. They reached a détente, which stemmed from Mark's relatively swift acceptance of Barney as a fact of life. Martha's total devotion to what he felt was a high-maintenance, not-very-lovable pet seemed a bit absurd, but so what? He was able to accept the absurd not only because he loved Martha but also because he had a strong enough sense of self to see that he and his wife were two distinct people. Barney was a small thorn in an otherwise happy life.

Several years into their marriage, Mark flew from their home in Baltimore to Houston to visit with family members and old friends. Shortly after he arrived, Martha called. She was crying so hard he could barely understand her. Yet she did manage to convey to him that Barney had taken ill. He had a serious malignancy, which had spread quickly. The vet had recommended euthanasia.

Barney had been unusually quiet the past few weeks, Mark reflected, and had shown little interest in food. Now it was all beginning to make sense. As Martha wept into the phone, Mark comforted her as best as he could. After they said goodnight, he settled into bed in his brother's guest room and thought about his wife, half a country away from him and all alone with a dying pet, her beloved companion of many years. *What a heartbreaking time for her*, he thought. Yet she hadn't asked him to come home.

Martha, he knew, was fiercely independent for a reason. When she was eight years old, her father had died suddenly, and her mother had retreated into such deep grief that the little girl had no choice but to rely on herself. By the time Mark met her, she was so self-reliant that he was hard-pressed to find ways to support her. Now here was a way. He called her back.

"I'm flying home tomorrow," he told her.

Mark made his decision freely, unhampered by guilt or duty — either of which might have morphed into resentment later. Instead, Mark acted from a strong sense of self, which enabled him to make clear distinctions between his own feelings and someone else's, an ability at the core of differentiation. He didn't like Barney — he was, in fact, relieved and even elated that the dog would soon be gone. But he deeply loved Martha. He could stretch generously for his wife's sake without sharing her pain himself.

How did Mark reach a place where he could remain so different from Martha and yet cross over into her world to offer support and care when she needed it? The key was that he'd built a strong foundation for himself before he met Martha. After falling in love with her, he continued to nourish his personal aims alongside those he shared with Martha — practicing guitar, keeping up with his golf game, and staying in touch with his college friends. His ability to strike a balance between his life as an individual and his life as a partner allowed him to give back to Martha generously and willingly.

One Wild and Precious Life

"Tell me, what is it you plan to do / with your one wild and precious life?" This question appears at the end of Mary Oliver's poem "Summer Day."[1] When I last checked, that phrase produced more than two million Google results, with links to websites and blogs, all of which referenced that "one wild and precious life." Clearly, the phrase has tapped into something universal.

Whether or not we're part of a couple, we come into the world alone, we leave alone, and we make many of our most important decisions after we've done our own private soul-searching. We and we alone are responsible for our behavior; we create our own lives. It behooves us, then, to build within ourselves a foundation that does honor to our life, which indeed is wild, precious, and unlike any other.

Let's examine how we might nourish this priceless natural resource.

Three Essential Questions

In my work with couples over the years, I've found that exploring three essential questions enables us to master the art of differentiation in much the way Mark did with Martha — and with similar results as a person and as a partner. Our answers change as the seasons of our lives change, so we will ask them more than once. The core questions are these:

Where have I been?
Where am I now?
Where am I going?

Each question naturally flows from the other: (1) exploring *where we've been* should give us enough self-awareness and information to (2) assess *where we are now* and to see how much, or how little, progress we've made toward our ideas of fulfillment. When we ask this second question, it's time to consider whether or not our ideas of success still make sense to us. The monk and mystic Thomas Merton was thought to have said, "People may spend their whole lives climbing the ladder of success only to find, once they reach the top, that the ladder is leaning against the wrong wall." Many of the first big decisions we make in life arise either out of opposition to or in compliance with our caretakers and authority figures. Some of us reach the top of Merton's ladder before we realize it isn't really where we want to be.

Once we've taken stock, we're ready to (3) consider *where we're going* next. As we ponder this issue, we might consider: What is my gift to contribute? What is my heart's desire? If we do decide to head in a new direction, we need to be intentional, determined, and prepared to succeed.

Let's look at each of these fundamental questions in more detail.

Where Have I Been?

To understand ourselves and our place in the world, we need to become aware of the influence of family members, including ones we've never met.

Home is where we first learn about relationships: how people care and repair, get their needs met, deal with disappointment and trouble, and find — or don't find — support. Within the family circle, some individuals influence us more than others. Most people assume that we're most deeply influenced by our parents, but some of us are more affected by relationships with other family members, such as siblings or grandparents.

Family is also where we learn about emotions. Our early experiences shape our sense of self-worth and our feelings about our competence and lovability. We're taught values and receive messages (many of them unspoken) about sexuality, money, support, conflict, differences of opinion, and what it takes to be safe and loved. It's in those early years that many of us are introduced to the demon of shame, which can impair our well-being and sense of possibility.

It's also during childhood that we discover our affinity to certain frames of mind. Some of us are born dreamers, drawn to possibilities, while others like to organize and systemize what is already here. We discover our own special joys, whether they lie in the natural wonders of clouds and trees, in music and drawing, or in the mathematical beauty of building and engineering. If we're lucky, these early affinities develop into adult passions and/or professions.

My husband's earliest memories are rooted in the wildlife in his parents' backyard garden. "I was invariably curious about what I'd find there," he told me. "So I went out and explored almost as soon as I could walk. I found worms and snails, hedgehogs and nesting birds. Straightaway, I was hooked." That early fascination led him to raise mice, save strays, and read every book on animals that he could find. His parents showed an ongoing interest in his creatures; his father helped build cages and pens, his mother fed his mice and kittens when he was in school. His decision to become a veterinarian was a natural outcome of this early exposure to animal life, and he never doubted his path. Had he been raised in another kind of family — with parents, say, who were shopkeepers and expected him to join the family business — this love of animals might've remained dormant, perhaps emerging for the first time in midlife when he realized that the ladder was leaning against the wrong wall.

For many of us, however, the "right wall" isn't clear. We can't remember what filled our hearts with desire as children, and we stumble in search of a meaningful life and vocation. To regain our sense of where we've been, and of what sparks our joy, we might try to determine when we stopped feeling engaged in life. Cultural anthropologist Angeles Arrien reminds us that wise humans have long recognized the revelations to be had in the recovery of such moments, which lie lodged in our memories: "In many shamanic societies, if you came to a shaman or medicine person complaining of being disheartened, dispirited, or depressed, they would ask you one of four questions: When did you stop dancing? When did you stop singing? When did you stop being enchanted by stories? When did you stop finding comfort in the sweet territory of silence?"[2]

We are shaped by both the light and the dark. As children we experienced and remember certain things that heartened us: our friends, say, or a loving pet, or a special teacher. Other things may have harmed us: bullying, lack of connection with one parent or both, or other trauma. Teasing may have stopped us from dancing and singing and caused us to lose our sense of enchantment. At other times, whole new possibilities may have arisen, perhaps allowing us to blossom for the first time.

Some of our formative events may have happened long ago to our ancestors, not to us personally. Immigration, financial upheaval, religious persecution, and wartime hardships are but a few of the circumstances whose profound effects are passed on from one generation to the next. Eva Fogelman, a clinical psychologist, believes that even third-generation Holocaust survivors experience some of the effects of that trauma, including low self-esteem, difficulty with trust, and a need for financial security that cannot be fulfilled. Of course, the upside of survival may also be passed on through generations, including resilience and determination to make the most of one's life.

For better and for worse, then, our family experience has a powerful impact on our personalities, sensitivities, strengths, and weaknesses. Yet we needn't remain at the mercy of our history. As we grow older, our answers to the question, "Where have I been?" can liberate us, especially since the clues we need to resolve current problems often point backward, as they did for two clients of mine.

Joe and Victoria, each in a second marriage, had been together for eighteen years when they first came to my office. They claimed to be happy but for one maddening and seemingly insoluble problem.

"All I ask is for her to show up when she says she's going to," Joe explained. "But she just won't do it. Why can't she be on time?" His voice was full of distress.

Victoria sat beside her husband, her mouth a tight line. Her eyes blazed with anger. "I've worked on this," she snapped. "I'm almost always on time now, but it's still not good enough. If I'm one minute late, he explodes. It's gotten to be such a big deal that I don't want to come home anymore."

A heavy silence followed.

"Maybe each of you could restate the problem as you see it," I suggested. "Let's think of this session as a sort of excavation. Dig down through the layers, if you will. Joe, let's start with you. How do you feel when Victoria is late?"

"I feel dissed," he said, "like she has no respect for me."

Victoria jumped in. "*You* don't feel respected! How do you think I feel, when you shout at me if I'm three seconds behind schedule?"

"Yes, but there I am — expecting to see you — and you're not there," Joe said. "It just about kills me."

The level of pain in Joe's voice got my attention. "Let's concede that being on time is important, Joe. Is it possible, however, that you feel a lot more upset than the situation calls for?"

Joe shrugged. "Yeah, I can see where you might think I'm overreacting. But the thing is, for me, it really is anguish, and Vikki ought to understand that by now."

"Never mind what your wife should or shouldn't know, Joe," I said. "Let's just focus on you for the moment." He nodded.

"My hunch is that there may be some other reason why this situation isn't merely annoying but deeply upsetting to you," I said. "Could there be any truth in this hunch, Joe? Is there maybe something else besides Victoria's lateness that makes you feel so much distress — maybe even fear?"

"Fear?" he shot back. "It's got nothing to do with fear!"

"Just take a breath," I told Joe gently, "and let's give this idea a chance. Is there anything about this situation with Victoria that reminds you of things that happened to you in the past?"

"Of course not!" he snapped.

I pressed on. "I mean someone being late, and your worrying?"

Joe took a few more deep breaths. Clearly it was hard for him to get underneath his fury, but he hung in there.

"Okay, maybe it hurts because she doesn't care enough about me to do this — this one simple thing," he admitted. "But I don't know about fear. What does that have to do with anything?"

I said nothing and just nodded.

Joe didn't say anything, either, and the room went quiet for a while. Then his impatience gave way to surprise, and his face crumpled.

"My mother," he said. He paused for a long time before he could go on. "My mother, she didn't come home." His voice sounded far away, and his eyes seemed to fix on something beyond my office.

"One day — I was about seven, I guess," he began slowly, and then the story spilled out of him. "My mother went shopping and left me with the housekeeper. She was supposed to come home by four. Well, she didn't return, and she didn't call. My father came home from work, and still she didn't show. Finally, after dark, there was a knock at the door; it was the police. She'd been in an accident."

Joe's mother had survived but suffered a serious spinal injury. A few weeks later, his parents decided to send him to a military school, which, for a young boy in the 1950s, was a lonely and unforgiving place. He was simply told it was "for the best," and he didn't question, protest, or grieve. His exile from home was never discussed again.

Now, five decades later, as he sat there in my office, tears began to roll down his face. Victoria moved her chair closer to his; she, too, was crying. They embraced for a long moment. Then Joe said to his wife, "I do want you to be on time. But when you're late, I also worry that — that something is wrong." His voice broke again.

From the outset of our session, the energy of Joe's distress appeared to be far greater than the circumstances warranted. In my Love Cycles workshop, we call this reaction an "80–20," a situation that merits an annoyance level of about 20 percent but is met with 100 percent distress. The explanation for the difference between the appropriate 20 percent response and the remaining 80 percent can be found somewhere in our history. This dynamic is also sometimes called an "emotional allergy."[3]

This kind of allergy is an exaggerated reaction, a sign that the immediate situation has triggered something that is old, painful, and unresolved. Joe's memory linked his wife's lateness with long-ago trauma, which also had involved waiting for an important woman in his life to arrive. Although he wasn't conscious of this association, he did feel a redoubled intensity of his emotions. Like many men, Joe found it easier to feel and express anger than fear.

If we don't understand what drives us, we think it's all about our partner's actions, and she, alas, will bear the brunt of all our raw, unprocessed misery. Once Victoria heard Joe's story, however, she stopped feeling like a chastised child. She understood what drove his disproportionate reaction to her tardiness. "Joe," she said, pressing his hand, "from now on, I won't just try. I'll make it my first priority to be on time."

For his part, Joe was astonished that something that had happened so long ago could play such a powerful role in his life now. "I didn't know it was so important. I'd even forgotten about it," he said, shaking his head in wonderment. "How could I have an advanced degree, run a company, and fly my own plane and not see what a world of worry I was still carrying around from when I was a boy?"

For me, the session also underscored how critical it can be to hear our partner out. If Joe and Victoria had merely continued to trade barbs, they might never have unearthed the story that lay beneath their problem. Although discovering the root of the problem does not make it go away, the awareness of it gives us new choices. Joe's first instinct when Victoria is late may always be distress, but now he has a choice to react from his old place of fear and anger or to respond from the new one with curiosity and calm.

Although we may not have such a dramatic story hidden in our own psyches, we all have triggers. As with Joe, some of these triggers lie below our consciousness, just waiting to be set off by our partner's inadvertent words or behavior. If we can dig beneath the layers of our histories, however, and listen openly and compassionately to each other, we can begin to live in "real time," both with our partners and with ourselves.

Where Am I Now?

Who hasn't awakened in the middle of the night, wondering, "What am I doing with my life?" Who hasn't had doubts about their line of work and wondered what it would've been like to have followed the "road not taken"? Being in tune with ourselves is a prerequisite to being in harmony with another. Even as we work on our relationship, each of us needs to make the time to reflect on the deep questions that human beings have asked for centuries: Who am I? What is my life about? How do I express my core values? Where do I put my time, energy, and money — and what do I get back in return? Does my work make sense to me? Where does my passion lie? What am I building? What will I leave behind after I die?

These were questions that Megan and Charlie began to ask themselves during the time that I worked with them. Megan had continued to rise in her career in health-care administration. By now she was near the top of her corporation's hierarchy. While she took satisfaction in her upward mobility, she also suffered from chronic anxiety. When she reflected on her past, she began to understand her lifelong need for approval and the goal that accompanied it — doing everything perfectly. Despite all her outward success, this twin desire for approval and perfection made her feel fundamentally powerless. Before each evaluation or promotion, she felt painfully fragile.

Megan already had come to understand how much her fling with James had been motivated by her desire to rebel against her belief that she needed to be perfect for the sake of every-one around her. "It may have been the most selfish choice I ever made," she told me one day, "but it was the first time in my life I didn't worry about having to earn love. I felt like I could just be me." This insight into her early needs allowed her to soften and develop some compassion for the vulnerable little girl who still lived inside her.

In a session one day she shared with us that, from a very early age, she had developed a rich fantasy life that gave her the freedom to be whoever she wanted to be. Sometimes she would comply with her parents' demands on her not just to *do* her best but to *be* the best, while, at the same time, she would dwell in her private fantasy world.

"What was that like?" I asked.

"I invented a whole life. I was a princess in Japan, and I built up a kingdom, even down to my favorite koi fish." She laughed. "His name was Harold, and he would talk to me when I was sad. I also had a secret life at school. I always had at least one friend my parents would've disapproved of, if they'd known. Like Meredith, whose parents were seldom home. We would sit in her living room eating junk food and watching soap operas, neither of which would have been tolerated by my parents."

Her recollections seemed to animate her. "I really want to loosen up," she told me one day. "I need to find things that I love to do, just for me."

To hear Megan express an interest in expanding her life was encouraging. I never would have guessed, however, that a woman as reserved as she was would take up the martial art aikido. She noticed a flyer at her health club and soon was attending two or three classes a week. "I've never felt so alive in my adult life," she told me, "so comfortable in my own skin."

Freed from her role as a "model woman," Megan grew even bolder. As a child, she'd loved horseback riding but gave it up as a teenager after her parents had discouraged it as "tomboyish."

Now she found a quality stable nearby, took some refresher lessons, and began to ride regularly. To everyone's surprise, she took her first vacation alone, at a dude ranch in Wyoming.

That autumn, Charlie had a serious bicycle accident in which he fractured his wrist and broke a clavicle. Although he was expected to make a full recovery, while recuperating he became deeply depressed. As he convalesced, he felt that Megan did everything "wrong": she pampered him, gave him endless pep talks about the "glass being half-full," and searched the Internet for the latest treatments for broken collarbones.

The hard work they had done to repair their marriage paid off, however. When Charlie asked Megan to stop coddling him, she did, remembering that "I'm not you" and "you're not me." Charlie then chose his own recovery mode, which was resting alone in a darkened room with a glass of water on the bedside table and ESPN, the TV sports channel, on all day at low volume. Once he was back on his feet, Charlie asked Megan to let him continue to manage his convalescence his own way. She was able to hear him. "I'm here if you need me," she told him simply.

Charlie spent a lot of time walking in the woods during his recovery, where he mulled over the questions of where he'd been and where he was now. He thought about his unhappiness and admitted to himself that his depression hadn't stemmed just from his accident; he'd been feeling blue for the past few years. Then he had a revelation: he'd devoted his whole life to trying to fix people, not only in body but in mind and spirit, too. Long before he learned medicine, he'd learned how to soothe away conflict.

As a child, he'd seen the unhappiness in his mother's eyes and done his best to keep the household quiet and peaceful. Among his three brothers, he was the peacemaker, the one who tried to prevent further derailments in a family that had already endured some serious ones. He got the best grades he could, excelled at farm work and school sports, and became skilled at talking his hot-tempered brothers out of fighting with one another.

Later, when he worked as a physician in Sudan, he set an unrelenting schedule for himself. The heartbreak he felt witnessing HIV deaths, lack of medication for treatable illnesses like malaria and even worms, and the wide-eyed sorrow of the children spurred him to travel to more villages, visit more orphanages, treat more sick people. When he returned to the States, he was driven by the same urge to "fix" and settled into a sixty-hour-a-week medical practice. Now, decades later, the emotional toll of seeing sick kids all day long had caught up with him. He was thoroughly burned-out.

As he began to consider new options, he asked Megan for her support. She gave it readily. "It wasn't hard to give him the time and space to figure things out for himself," said Megan. "I'm a whole lot more relaxed than I used to be. I don't need Charlie to answer to me constantly anymore, or to stay glued to one spot."

Where Am I Going?

We all need to look ahead. To the best of our ability, we need first to imagine, and then to plot, our course for the future. Of course, there are no guarantees that we'll get to where we're headed. As the filmmaker Woody Allen has said, "If you want to make God laugh, tell him your plans." Still, it is useful to ask ourselves: What is it time to let go of? What is it time to begin to build? Reflecting on these questions will help us find the path that will take us forward.

Eventually, Charlie made his move. He left patient care and became a consultant to other doctors and went on to teach in medical school. No longer on call, he had the free time to discover what else gave him joy in life. He rediscovered his love for guitar, took up fly-fishing, planted a big vegetable garden in the backyard, and bought six plump hens to supply his family with fresh eggs.

As Charlie described his new life to me, Megan shrieked in mock horror: "Look who we've become, Charlie — a karate woman and a chicken farmer!"

They smiled in mutual tolerance — *masters of the art of differentiation*, I thought. Both Megan and Charlie had given themselves permission to become themselves, and their pact of authenticity had become a core part of their relationship. As they became more real in themselves, they became more real to each other and to others. They found ways to enjoy new activities together, including horseback riding on the weekends and a new-found shared love of yoga. Their social life began to expand, too, as they made new friends with whom they could share a larger sense of themselves.

Yet they continued to prize their differences, and for good reason. As psychologist Esther Perel has written so perceptively, "Space invites otherness and differences....In order to have wanting, we need the sense of mystery, a bridge to cross and someone to visit on the other side."[4] Once upon a time, Megan and Charlie felt that they knew each other inside out. Now they were intrigued to find out that they didn't. Charlie's "backyard farming" led him to a passion for exotic cooking, and Megan was amazed that Mr. Meat and Potatoes had learned how to cook vegan meals that were really delicious. When Megan worked out in the aikido dojo and Charlie saw his once buttoned-down wife come home sweaty and messy, he found it a surprising turn-on. "Who the hell *is* this woman?" he wondered, smiling to himself.

During their final visit to my office, the couple announced that they would soon take off on a horseback-riding tour of the Clare Burren Trail in Galway, Ireland, to celebrate their seventeenth anniversary. What a long way these two had come — through all five stages of love. At first, they had merged deeply, each certain that they'd found their "missing half." Later, they felt like they knew each other all too well and became aware of the many ways they *didn't* fit together. They began to move apart, feeling that they had little in common except for exasperation and irritation. Megan's relationship with James brought them to the darkest moment of their marriage; for a while, Charlie's anger over the betrayal and Megan's shame threatened to take over. Their decision to find their way back to each other and to build a new partnership had met with success, largely because each had squarely faced those crucible moments and been willing to go through all the stages of healing. Having grown both together and individually, they are now able to enjoy their relationship while also pursuing separate interests that are vital to each. They are fully savoring their conscious marriage during the times it is thriving and have developed the tolerance and goodwill to carry them through when it is faltering.

Why the Three Questions Are Essential

Where have I been? Where am I now? Where am I going? Charlie and Megan asked and answered these necessary questions, and as their lives continue, they can expect to do so again from time to time. What makes these questions so crucial?

To ask the question, "Where have I been?" grounds us in place and time and allows us to understand our nature and psyche. To ask, "Where I am now?" allows us to assess where we are in our journey of self-discovery, which is the primary work of our lives. "Where am I going?" speaks to change, which is a constant and reflects the human search for meaning.

As stated above, part of the significance of these three questions is how each one leads naturally to the next. If we can understand where we've come from, including the dreams we may have put away and the roads we may not have taken, then we can begin to look at where we are now. Once we reflect on and understand what does and doesn't work in our present lives, we can begin to get a fair idea of what's next for us. Gradually, we will expand and develop into the whole, self-actualizing person we're meant to be, someone who is prepared to be a mature, openhearted partner to another human being. As we begin to balance the legitimate needs of both self and other in a continuous, conscious dance, we practice the vital art of differentiation.

Chapter Ten

WHOLEHEARTED LOVING
The Barriers

*Your task is not to seek for love,
but merely to seek and find all the barriers within yourself
that you have built against it.*

— attributed to JALALUDDIN RUMI

When they walked into my office for our first session, Jason and Melissa looked glum. Jason plopped down in the middle of the couch, while Melissa edged over to one end, practically perching on the sofa's arm.

Jason sighed heavily. "For a long time, we've been feeling kind of numb to each other," he said. "You know: the kids, work — everything gets in the way of our relationship. Finally, we talked about it."

Staring at the floor, Melissa spoke up: "Jason said he'd read somewhere that going away together could be good for a marriage," she said, her voice flat. "It was fine with me, because I really needed a break. The kids were going to camp for two weeks, so we bought tickets to Hawaii and took off."

"Right," Jason chimed in, "off to connect and play!" Now he sounded sarcastic, even disdainful. "For ten days, Melissa read romance novels and sat by the pool. I begged her to have some fun with me. 'Let's play some golf,' I suggested. 'Or how about we take a swim — in the pool or the ocean — your choice.'" He snorted in disgust. "I even had the nerve to suggest we go back to our room after lunch and make love. Nothing doing. She wouldn't budge from her lounge on the patio. She slept late, so I ate breakfast alone, and we hardly spoke over dinner. What a recharge!"

Melissa twisted toward him, her fists clenched in anger. "Right, Jason. I went away on my 'big trip' to Hawaii to feel even more pressure than I do at home to do what everyone else wants. I'm the one who gave up her career to stay at home with the kids, and sometimes I feel like I have totally lost myself. I am simply a schedule manager and driver for our children's soccer and swimming events." She exhaled a long, loud breath. "Do you even see me? I don't think you said one personal thing to me the whole time; you just wanted me to do, do, do!"

Sadly, I hear this vacation story all too often. Couples get the message from magazines, TV programs, well-meaning friends, and even counselors that their best bet is to go have some fun together — on a date, a weekend getaway, or even a long holiday — to rekindle their spark through play and relaxation.

Play, however, is a trickier marital aid than we might imagine, as we'll discuss in more depth in the next chapter.

With Jason and Melissa there was no meeting of the minds. His suggestions to play golf or swim simply didn't appeal to his wife. Her idea of fun in the sun was simply to escape a daily life that she found burdensome, full of drudgery and obligation. What she wanted and needed was to just sit poolside and vegetate, enjoying the sun's warmth seeping into her tight, tense body. At the same time, she was stonewalling her husband, because she harbored deep frustration and anger with respect to their domestic routine. Although she had agreed to take some years off her work as a high school English teacher, she had grown quickly bored with her homebound routine and missed the intellectual stimulation and friendship at work. Some days she couldn't remember what she had done with her time in the past twenty-four hours, but she was tired a lot and sick of the assumptions her family made that she would manage the family logistical details since she was "the one at home." Sometimes she felt envious of the fast pace and constant travel of Jason's engineering position in a small start-up. *Never mind what Jason wants,* she thought bitterly on the trip. *He can find his own fun.*

He didn't find it, of course. He was miserable, lonely, and angry, as well as oblivious to his wife's real needs and desires. Although ostensibly the two spent an enviable ten days in Hawaii, they actually sat out their vacation on either side of a barricade.

The problems that lay behind the barrier were ones that the couple needed to address and resolve before they would be ready to play. Melissa needed to reassess her life and decide whether her decision to stay at home was still working for her. They needed to make some new agreements about shared responsibilities and look at the sources of Melissa's resentment and Jason's sense of distance between them. If their trip to Hawaii was far from a dream vacation, at least it clarified the work this couple needed to do, beginning with an honest conversation.

The Gateway to Wholehearted Loving

For the two of us to merely exist as a couple, we don't have to be open or vulnerable with our partner. But if we want to share a genuine, vibrant emotional connection, we do have to let down our guard and show up as the person we truly are. To recognize, examine, and talk about our feelings is how we begin to understand and care for ourselves — and, in turn, how we begin to understand and cherish those we love.

Some of us see vulnerability as a weakness. By definition it means that we open ourselves to the possibility of damage or pain. Of course, some types of vulnerability can expose us to grave harm — common sense tells us not to walk down a dark alley at night or to reveal our deepest secrets to someone whom we know to be untrustworthy. However, taking the risk to be vulnerable in our most intimate relationship gives us the opportunity to become more wholehearted with our partner and ourselves. At the same time, it takes a brave and trusting heart to open up to, and own, the person you are. It requires courage to accept your strengths and your weaknesses in equal measure, and to register your experience simply as it lands, without the need to spin your story to protect yourself. You don't need to stage-manage how others see you — or how you see yourself — but letting go of this role requires healthy self-esteem.

During the first stage, love disarmed us. As we merged with our partner, being vulnerable felt easy and natural. We accepted his idiosyncrasies, supported his dreams, shared our secrets, and opened ourselves to play and passion. Since then, we've moved through Doubt and Denial, Disillusionment, and Decision — and we can't go back the way we came.

The goal in this fifth stage — wholehearted loving — is to regain the joy of the first stage but without the help of the love drug that once made openness and generosity so effortless. The only way to regain some of the original magic of our early days together is to create a new partnership — one that is grounded in wholeheartedness.

If we're in a relationship and choose to recommit in the fifth stage, we do so with the awareness that our partner won't meet all our needs. Further, we understand that we carry within us enough resources to take care of ourselves. We no longer feel the desperation often associated with romantic love — the fearful conviction that I'm nothing without you and that I need to do whatever I can to be sure you'll always love me.

To love wholeheartedly means that I care and give without trying to fix you, change you, or make you see how indispensable and wonderful I am. I have no agenda except to respond to you from the best and most mature part of me.

The pursuit of wholeheartedness is not limited to couples who decide to enter the fifth stage, however. We are surrounded by cultural imperatives that insist we need to meet the "right person" before we can become wholehearted. Not so! You are the right person, and the only person, who can take on this task for yourself. An ongoing relationship offers a good training ground, but so do all our relationships. Wholehearted loving is available to us all, whether we are single or romantically involved.

Blocks and Barriers

While the steps that lead us toward wholehearted loving are straightforward, they can be challenging because of the obstacles we've put in our way. Barriers to wholeheartedness vary in their intensity and commonality. We'll look at several in this chapter. Regardless of the kind of obstacles we confront, however, we need to realize that they block our joy as much as they block our pain. If we are to experience genuine, openhearted delight and trust, we need to dismantle them.

To begin, we must find the courage to look inside ourselves, to reexamine the fears and limitations that grew out of certain experiences in our lives. We need to get behind the barriers themselves and examine the old wounds that fester there. We need to recognize them with compassion so that we can understand why we built a wall to protect ourselves in the first place. If we fail to take this step, we can't truly heal our relationship or ourselves. This is how my clients Jason and Melissa got stuck — they tried to find a solution before they recognized the problem.

The Barrier of Codependence

One obstacle that often stands in the way of wholeheartedness is the entanglement known as "codependence," in which we try to control another person by changing our own boundaries to suit her, denying our own truth to please her, or hiding our distress about some aspects of the relationship so we won't upset her. Let's look at how we behave if we aren't codependent but instead maintain firm, healthy boundaries:

- I recognize my own bottom line (things I need that aren't negotiable), but I'm willing to cooperate on all other aspects of my life with my partner. Sometimes this means I'll carry a bigger load than I usually do.
- I recognize that each of us is a self-contained individual who brings his or her own distinct gifts to the union, and I believe that it's a fair exchange.
- My sense of self-worth, security, and well-being isn't tied up exclusively in the ebb and flow of my relationship; I possess the inner resources to be grounded within myself. Because I want to love, however, I remain as open and vulnerable as I can.
- I can tell the truth.

We develop wholeheartedness to realize ourselves fully, not to change another person or win his love. Codependence comes from a place of deficiency. Wholeheartedness arises out of abundance, which reflects an integrated, healthy self built on self-acceptance. We open ourselves to love our partner fully, but we don't need our partner to complete us. We are already whole.

The Barrier of Love Addiction

One of the barriers to real love is pervasive and not easy to overcome. It's the lure of fantasy love, which held us in its grip in the first stage. Romance is a seductive siren song, but it can distract us from true love. We must let it go so that our love can be reborn in a form that is more whole.

The visceral pull of romance makes it hard to kick. In chapter 1, we looked at the ways in which romantic love is mediated by biochemical changes and how our emotional responses are similar to those associated with addiction.

- Your partner boosts your mood when he acts lovingly toward you; your mood crashes when he doesn't.
- You sacrifice time, which you used to spend with friends and family, so that just the two of you can be together.
- Your lover feels like your very salvation. You break your own rules to please her.
- You stifle your feelings and needs and preferences to ensure the most positive response from your partner.

As a matter of fact, according to the scientists who have studied it, romantic love really is an addiction. Helen E. Fisher, a biological anthropologist at Rutgers University and the author of *Why We Love*, explains: "It's a very powerfully wonderful addiction when things are going well and a perfectly horrible addiction when things are going poorly."[1] And "Romantic love is not an emotion.... It's a drive. It comes from the motor of the mind, the wanting part of the mind, the craving part of the mind."[2]

No wonder we find the romance habit hard to kick. As we know very well by now, however, love's initial spell isn't sustainable any more than a drug's initial high is. Fortunately, as we've moved on through love's subsequent stages, we've grown in ways that will help us experience romance in a new way. We've confronted other obstacles that have held us back from engaging our hearts fully. Now we're ready to move forward, if we choose, to rebuild our lives with a person who won't meet all our needs but with whom we can discover what it means to love wholeheartedly.

The Barrier of a Closed Heart

Closing our hearts is a common reaction to the curve balls that life throws us. When our hearts feel broken, they tend to close up. Our hearts break when we feel betrayed or we are dumped by the love of our life. We endure it when our relationship is badly adrift and we don't know how to steer it back on course. How many hundreds of songs have found their way to fame because they speak to the universal sorrow of a broken heart? Billy Ray Cyrus sings of his "Achy Breaky Heart." Patsy Cline wails, "I Fall to Pieces," while Elvis croons about "Heartbreak Hotel." Steven Tyler of Aerosmith rocks out to "Hole in My Soul," while Toni Braxton begs of her dead lover, "Unbreak My Heart." Billie Holiday makes us cry when we hear "Good Morning Heartache."

When our hearts break, we are understandably disappointed, hurt, and angry. This anguish also registers in our body. There is a change in the blood flow in the brain, and the anterior cingulate cortex (responsible for the regulation of distress) becomes active. Recent MRI studies of subjects in the midst of a breakup revealed that the part of their brains that registered emotional rejection was the same part that reacted to severe pain.[3]

As Michael Ondaatje wrote in *The English Patient*, "The heart is an organ of fire."[4] The depression that can accompany heartbreak can also alter our physical sensations — the pleasure we take in touch, the taste of food, and even our sense of smell. As one of our culture's most lovable losers, cartoon character Charlie Brown, observed, "Nothing takes the taste out of peanut butter quite like unrequited love."

Once we are hurt this badly, many of us vow never to risk that kind of pain again — and therefore we shut down our hearts. We think doing so is a sign of wisdom. As actor Charlie Sheen has said, "The best way not to get your heart broken is to pretend you don't have one."

This doesn't necessarily mean that we avoid a new relationship because we have had a previous heartbreak, but if we do not allow ourselves the grief, and then the healing, from our old relationship, we cannot fully show up in the new one. We will always be too careful, suspicious, and withholding to let new love in.

The Barrier of Halfhearted Love

Some barriers to wholehearted love, although less traumatic than heartbreak, can have devastating consequences all the same. Certain sorts of inner blindness can cause us to love with only half a heart. Self-absorption can cause us to be only half-open to our partner's needs. As a consequence, our partner may reciprocate by loving us halfheartedly as well.

M. Scott Peck, psychiatrist and bestselling author of *The Road Less Traveled*, once wrote that love is "the will to extend one's self for the purpose of nurturing one's own or another's spiritual growth."[5]

Among other things, love means that we support our partner in her effort to do what's right by her lights, even if the consequences are annoying or difficult for us. Our loyalty isn't limitless, of course. It doesn't extend to actions we consider un-ethical or destructive.

Extending wholehearted love, of course, is easier said than done. But settling for less carries real hazards, as my clients Melanie and Drew discovered. The couple first came to see me to discuss Ashley, Drew's twelve-year-old daughter from his first marriage.

Melanie was the first to speak. As she did, she moved her hand up and down on the arm of the chair, as though to under-score every word.

"Ashley is rude to me," she began. "She gives me dirty looks when Drew isn't around. She disregards all our rules. She won't lift a hand to pick up a dirty plate, and she complains all the time about everything. The kid never has the right clothes for what-ever we have planned. If we tell her ahead of time that we're going to the pool, you can bet she'll show up without a swimsuit."

Melanie let out a deep sigh. "Things would be perfect if it wasn't for that child of his," she groused. "I wish we didn't have to see her so much. It's not like she gets much fun out of the time she spends with us, either, that's for sure."

As she talked, Drew slumped in his chair and wrapped his arms around his body as if to shield himself. His face tightened into a grimace. When at last Melanie had no more to say, he sat in silence for a moment, staring at the rug.

"I know Ashley can be difficult," he finally began. "The di-vorce was hard on her and now she's heading into her teens, which brings its own challenges. But she's really a great kid." His face lit up for a moment, and then sagged. "I don't want her to think I've abandoned her just because her mother and I couldn't make it."

Melanie scowled. "That's just what we don't need, Drew, a budding teenager who resents you and hates me. If you love me as much as you say you do, you'll lay it on the line: either she behaves, and does exactly what I tell her to around the house, or she can see you someplace else. Maybe for lunch somewhere."

I only saw the couple a few more times before Drew got a job offer that required a move across the country. Melanie insisted that he take the job and that they leave Ashley behind.

Drew complied. In a later phone session, he told me that he wasn't "stronghearted" enough to refuse his wife's demands. Neither he nor Melanie was "wisehearted" enough to realize how much their decision would cost them in the long run.

"I tried to split the difference," he explained, "but all I did was shortchange everyone. It'll probably take years to repair the damage I've done with Ashley."

The decision had an even more ruinous effect on the marriage. Drew's distance from his child was too high a price to pay. "I made a huge mistake," he said. "My guilt and resentment were too much for me to handle. It's what led to my breakup with Melanie."

After the couple's separation, Melanie came back to the area to live. She made an appointment with me to help her process all that had happened.

"I don't understand it," she said. "Everything was so good between us at first. He used to love to do things with me on the weekends. But after we moved, he'd just sit there like a lump. He wouldn't even remember to walk our dog. The man I married turned into someone else, someone who wasn't really there."

Drew had come to love her with only half a heart.

Melanie's attitude conveyed the inner blindness that can cause us to love with a possessive heart, when jealousy swamps us and we ignore our partner's needs. Once again, to love wholeheartedly is to want your partner to keep his important commitments, because it's through such commitments that he builds his

emotional and spiritual core. If I have to stop loving other people to love you (especially my children) my capacity to love will
shrink, not grow. Paradoxically, there will be less of me available
to love you.

The Barrier of the Stories We Tell Ourselves

Another sort of barrier to wholehearted love can arise out of the
false or incomplete stories we tell ourselves about our childhood
histories. Each time we relate this distorted narrative to ourselves
and others, we reinforce it further as the true story, along with
the true portrait of ourselves as the story's narrator. This is called
"confirmation bias."

A good example of confirmation bias can be found in the
story of my client Duane in chapter 6. Recall that I just "knew"
he'd be a man who hunted for the fun of it. When I spotted the
gun rack in his pickup truck, there was my proof. I'd already
formed a conclusion about this man's values, and then I jumped
on any evidence to support it. This kind of bias can also powerfully affect our recollections and beliefs about family history.
Family lore often arises out of our selective memories, and the
omissions, exaggerations, and distortions we make can wall us
off from reality. We may create a story so painful that it keeps us
from loving and trusting others.

When Steve first came to see me in therapy, his isolation
and sense of inadequacy had reached critical mass. His wife,
Stephanie, was considering separation, saying she'd rather live
alone than with someone as closed and unavailable as Steve was.
He spent hours in his shop or on the computer, rarely showed
up at their children's events, often missed dinner, and typically
responded to any question about how he was doing with, "Okay."

During my first few sessions with Steve, he said very little.
When I asked about his past, he said, "That's a black hole that I

don't want to go into." His family doctor, who had referred him, had sent me medical records showing that as a child, he'd been neglected by his mother and beaten and abused by his father. Both parents were alcoholics. As an adult, he was diagnosed with post-traumatic stress disorder. His medical records described him as "isolated, negative, and unhappy."

Shame dogged Steve, too. It stemmed from profound disgust with his image of himself and the family he came from. Like many children, his abuse had led him to conclude long ago that something must have been fundamentally wrong with him for him to have received such mistreatment. As Steve once blurted out to me, "I *am* something wrong."

Despite Steve's conviction of profound unworthiness, I observed many positive qualities in him. He showed up punctually and was easygoing and flexible when I had to reschedule. He had a sense of humor and a gentleness of spirit, and he seemed truly interested in finding out what he could do to get along better with his wife and children. All these positives gave me confidence that a door would open for us somewhere. Still, I was surprised when it turned out to be a secret love of birds, just as it had been with distressed Duane. I was reminded of a line from a poem by Jesuit priest and poet Gerald Manley Hopkins entitled "The Windhover": "My heart, in hiding, stirred for a bird."

Perhaps something about lightness or easy flight promised relief to these emotionally shuttered men. Maybe they saw birds as messengers from heaven, offering the possibility of a better world.

A few months into therapy, Steve seemed to forget now and then that he was supposed to be an introverted, laconic sort. In one session, he enthusiastically described how an acorn woodpecker leaped out of a eucalyptus tree to fly-catch.

"How did you come to learn so much about birds?" I asked.

"Oh, I've been paying attention to them as far back as I can remember," he said. "I knew a bunch of birdcalls by the time I was six. I remember in the late winter the owls would start up. I would listen to them when I had trouble sleeping or if I woke from a bad dream. There would always be one nearby in the big tree, and another one farther off."

Steve stopped then, as though he had exceeded his allotted time for speaking. "I'd love to hear more," I said.

"I didn't know it then, but it was the time of year when they were defending territories with their calls, near and far," he said. "In the spring, the robins were the first to start up in the morning, and the air was very cool so the sound traveled. And of course the blue jays, who came around to steal a few odd pieces of dog food from the porch." He grinned briefly at the memory. "In the fall were the geese. I knew they were leaving. Flying somewhere else."

In those few moments, Steve had spoken more words — and with more genuine engagement — than he had in any previous session. I knew there had to be more to his story than deprivation and misery. If we could find clues to the other side of his childhood, as he had shown me with his description of birdlife, maybe he could change his view of his story as an unmitigated "black hole."

I knew that photographs sometimes revealed things that people couldn't express in words. "Steve," I asked, "do you have any family photos from when you were a kid?"

"There's, uh, a box in the attic," he said haltingly. "I've never opened it." He shifted uncomfortably in his seat. "Frankly, I've never wanted to look inside."

But when he came to our next session, he was carrying the box. One of the first things we looked at together was a high school yearbook, dated 1941. Inside was a photo of Steve's father, an honor student in a letter sweater for his achievements in baseball. There, too, was his mother, homecoming queen and volleyball champion. They looked happy and relaxed. Nothing in the pictures hinted at dysfunction.

A stack of letters in the box revealed that Steve's parents got married right out of high school. World War II came along, and his father went off to Europe, leaving behind a pregnant wife. At nineteen, Steve's dad saw his entire battalion blown up, while back home his eighteen-year-old wife gave birth to a daughter so injured during the birth process that she couldn't speak, hear, or learn to feed herself.

After Steve's dad returned from the war, he was stationed on the West Coast. The letters revealed how overwhelmed they were by their daughter's limitations. She was plagued by seizures and cried continually. They reached the hard decision to place her in a state hospital. As was the custom in those days, parents were told not to visit. So they parted with their firstborn child forever.

Steve shook his head, stunned. "I had no idea." He was quiet for a moment. "They never said a thing about that baby."

"They were so young," I responded. "Without the skills or any support to care for her. They must've been hurt on so many levels."

The big cardboard box also held piles of family photos depicting picnics, birthday parties, and Christmas trees. Among the photos was a shot of Steve, about age six, with his mother. Together they are filling a bird feeder in the small wilderness of their overgrown backyard. In a companion photo, Steve watches as his father puts the finishing touches on an aviary he was constructing for his son. In the photo Steve is grinning from ear to ear. Here, at last, was evidence that Steve's parents had done something right.

Looking through the old Polaroids, Steve actually smiled. "I forgot all about these times," he said. "How could I do that? My memory is really terrible."

"Yes," I agreed. "Some of your memories really are terrible — so terrible that they wiped out all the good things that happened to you."

After spending several sessions going through the box, Steve and I reflected on what we'd seen and learned. All the things that Steve remembered were still true: his parents had been abusive, neglectful, and often drunk. Yet now we had some of the backstory, too. His parents had suffered a great deal: war trauma, the loss of their first child, and a move far from home. For the first time, Steve saw his parents in a more mixed light. Eventually, he'd rewrite his old narrative to accommodate this new information. His image of himself would change for the better, too. In the next chapter, we will look at how he changed his story and, in the process, became more wholehearted.

Skirmishing with Ghosts

In 1944 a young Japanese soldier named Hiroo Onoda received orders to report to Lubang, a remote island in the Philippines. There his secret mission was to spy on and disrupt anyone who was thought to be an enemy. His commanding officer ordered, "You are absolutely forbidden to die by your own hand. It may take three years, it may take five, but we'll come back for you. Until then, as long as you have one soldier, you must continue to lead him."

"Yes, sir," promised Onoda.

In the company of three other men, Onoda followed his commander's orders and lived on bananas, coconuts, and an occasional stolen cow. A year later, leaflets announcing the end of

World War II were air-dropped on the island. But the news made no difference to Onoda. He told his companions that he wouldn't consider his mission completed until he'd heard from his commander, to whom he had given his solemn word. He refused to budge. He and his soldiers continued to live in the mountains, fishing, stealing rice and chickens, and occasionally skirmishing with the local law-enforcement people. The Japanese government made repeated attempts to call Onoda and his companions back home. Thirty years passed, and finally his commander was located and sent to Lubang, where he read to Onoda the official orders to cease all combat activity. At last, Onoda laid down his weapons and returned to Japan.[6]

The Onoda Factor lives on, albeit in a different form. Tactics that once were an effective, even noble, way for us to deal with a situation become irrelevant and then counterproductive as facts and circumstances change. Yet we refuse to accept that the war is over, so to speak, and we keep up the fight. We skirmish with ghosts and become like ghosts ourselves, deprived of a life lived in real time.

I'm reminded of a client, Kathy, a schoolteacher who struggled with one failed relationship after another. Her mother died when she was nine, while her father, a former captain in the air force, treated his children much as he had his subordinates in the service. It fell to Kathy, the eldest child, to run the family: she cleaned, cooked, and took care of three younger siblings from the time she was ten years old. Her father demanded perfection in the execution of all her duties, on pain of shaming, shouting, and frequent corporal punishment. He allowed Kathy no dissent, no protest, and no signs of distress. The only acceptable response to his harshness was, "Yes, sir. I understand, sir. I'll do it immediately, sir." Kathy learned quickly to fulfill her father's expectations and to keep her inner thoughts and feelings invisible. Her behavior and attitude were totally appropriate, even wise, if she was to survive in this authoritarian environment.

As soon as she graduated from high school, Kathy left home. Yet the barriers she had built to cope with her father remained firmly in place. She continued to rely on the same combination of abject compliance and outward composure to interact with others. This behavior, which had served her so well, now stood in the way of any real connection with other people. Years later, when she came to see me, Kathy still had no idea how to establish warm and loving relations with other adults. Gradually, during two years of therapy, she began to surrender her old ways, becoming less unflappable and more real. She discovered an entire range of feelings, including anger, sorrow, and joy. She found a patient and loving partner who helped her begin the slow work of learning how to trust another person with all her emotions and of becoming vulnerable enough to give and receive love.

To some degree, the Onoda Factor operates in most of our lives. It's the basis of the dynamic I described in chapter 9 as an "80–20": a situation merits an annoyance level of about 20 percent, but we react to it with 100 percent distress. The explanation for the difference between the appropriate 20 percent response and the 80 percent overreaction can be found somewhere in our personal history.

The Onoda Factor is also the cornerstone of projection and transference, in which we respond to someone in the present moment as though he were a person from our past who had deeply influenced us. Kathy found that with her new partner, Jed, any expression of anger (even if it wasn't directed at her) caused her to feel startled and then afraid. It's difficult to overcome this hurdle because usually it occurs below our awareness level, and the first sign of its presence is relationship trouble.

Unfortunately, we often assume that the source of the trouble is our partner rather than the barriers we built long ago to protect ourselves from pain.

Love's Summit

We have spent most of this chapter looking at several kinds of barriers to wholehearted loving and some of the reasons we build them. The more familiar we are with these impediments, the easier it will be to dismantle them so that we can open ourselves to love at its fullest.

As we've discussed, vulnerability is the gateway to wholeheartedness. First, it leads to self-knowledge, which in turn opens us to a compassionate awareness of the feelings, thoughts, and experience of others. Once we pass through the gate, where do we head next? To answer this question, let's briefly retrace our steps.

When we first fell in love, it was as if we took a helicopter ride to the top of the Himalayas, the most spectacular mountains in the world. There we stood, awed by our new, rarified surroundings. We might've felt dizzy, breathless, nearly overtaken with wonder. We might also have felt delight at our luck and dazzled with possibility.

Yet we couldn't stand still and sustain that early sense that we two were merged and made whole. Inevitably, we had to return to ourselves.

Now we had to climb the mountains from base camp, step by treacherous step. The terrain was filled with obstacles, both those presented by the mountains themselves and those we erected ourselves. Along the way we slipped and stumbled into unseen crevices. At times we lost our way or found ourselves stuck in terrifying weather conditions — high winds, blinding snowstorms, bitter cold. We might have faltered and turned back. We might've decided that all the effort involved wasn't worth the risk — that the relationship was already too flimsy or too damaged to continue fighting for. Alternatively, we might've fallen and been injured in our attempt to scale the heights. Whatever the case, we struggled with uncertainty, fear, pain, confusion, and dread.

If we kept trudging up the mountain, however, we continued to explore. Eventually, we used both our own inner strength and the strengths of our partnership to fortify ourselves, and found ways to overcome or compensate for our weaknesses so that we could grow — whether together or apart.

If we continue now to ascend toward the summit, we may begin to realize that the trek itself offers us lessons that no other instruction can provide. It's through our daily climb, our repeated practice, that we truly stand the best chance to become wholehearted lovers. If we do, we'll find the rewards infinitely more worthwhile than they were in the first stage of love, and the view from the top far more exhilarating.

Once we achieve openheartedness with one person, we become more open to others, too. Our sensitivity to the needs of other people expands. We find it easier to be generous and to let go of grudges. We can do these things because we've broken down barriers and loosened our defenses. The world's great spiritual traditions impart a similar wisdom: our daily lives are the place to practice wholeheartedness in an impermanent, imperfect world.

As you continue to climb the mountain, remember that perfection isn't your goal. In fact, it's within the cracks and the crevices that you will find the light that leads to the freedom to be openhearted. In the last verse of his song "Anthem," poet and songwriter Leonard Cohen captures beautifully how we mend and heal: "There is a crack, a crack in everything / That's how the light gets in."

Light can be found in the cracks and crevices of the barriers we dismantle in ourselves, too. As we uncover this light within, we'll move forward toward the bridges that carry us into wholeheartedness.

Chapter Eleven

WHOLEHEARTED LOVING
The Bridges

Genuine love is between two people who know
they are already complete. Genuine love is based on a new paradigm
in which both partners are committed to the celebration
of each other and their loved ones.

— GAY HENDRICKS AND KATHLYN HENDRICKS, *Lasting Love*

In the last chapter, we discussed the inner work required to break down the barriers that shut us down and separate us from ourselves and our partners. To open our hearts again we begin to build the bridges that will take us toward a wholeness of heart. We fashion these bridges by practicing real acceptance of our partner and ourselves. We construct them out of the virtues extolled in the world's spiritual teachings — compassion, humor, humility, gratitude, generosity, and patience.

Indeed, the quest for wholeheartedness can be seen as something like a spiritual pilgrimage. But that doesn't mean our progress through the fifth stage is some somber, stately procession toward mature acceptance — or at least that's not all it is. It can also be a thrilling adventure. A number of tools are at our disposal for building bridges to one another in ordinary, everyday ways that can be fun, joyous, and spirited. This chapter describes some of them.

The Power of the Heart

I still have it, a faded card with a picture of a German shepherd (who looks a lot like Rin Tin Tin) on the front. The dog lies next to a big red pillow with "Happy Valentine's Day" written across it in yellow ink, banner style. Inside, even more thrilling, is the message: "love ya," in a boy's scrawling hand with a tiny heart alongside the signature, "Tony."

This card was hand-delivered to me with a Russell Stover marshmallow chocolate heart, wrapped in red tinfoil, when I was twelve years old. I felt like I would float away with joy. I read the brief message over and again and slept with the card near my pillow. I was convinced that the words *love ya* meant that fourteen-year-old Tony would be my true love — forever.

A few blissful months later, he called out of the blue to give me the following message: "I found out you're only twelve. The end," he hissed and hung up. So ended my first romance. His message stung me for a long, long time.

Although I still slept with his Valentine, the card's meaning changed. It became an emblem of everlasting tears and sorrow, in memory of a love that came so happily into my life and then departed so sadly. Almost fifty-eight years later, that card falls out occasionally from a book of love poems to remind me of that mysterious bundle of pleasure, yearning, and pining that we claim is our heart.

Our attraction to romantic love is boosted by the power of the heart as a symbol of love. The ecstasy of our early enthrallment is reinforced by the enduring power of this association.

The heart is the most important organ in our body. It's the life muscle that delivers oxygen to the brain and body, helps the body get rid of waste, and pumps blood to and from our lungs. We can live without a brain longer than we can live without a heart. Breathing, which is the first thing we do when we're born into the world and the last thing we do before we leave it, is a capacity that comes courtesy of our heart.

Perhaps it's because of the heart's location at the core of our bodies and its crucial purposes that we've adopted it as our symbol to describe our strongest feelings of affection, tenderness, attraction, and longing. The heart is the shape we draw in the sand to signify romance and affection. It's the red logo on cards, candy, balloons, and lockets that conveys "I love you." It adorns the language of poems, songs, epics, and stories. It even turned up as a small, red shape on a cave wall in Asturias, Spain, some twelve thousand years ago, according to writer Gail Godwin.[1]

References to the human heart also have religious and spiritual connotations, which are universal and timeless. In *The Sacred Heart of the World*, David Richo informs us:

> There are more than one thousand instances of the word *heart* in the Bible.... The human heart in Hindu tradition is called *Bramapura*, the abode of Brahma the creator. The heart has perennially represented centricity since it is the center of the body.... To the Chinese, the heart in the human body mirrors the position of the sun in the universe.... In Islam, the heart (*qalb*) stands for contemplation, spiritual life, and the connection between spirit and matter.... The symbol of the Sufi Order is a heart with wings. The heart is considered to be both earthly and heavenly.[2]

One of the best examples of the heart's use as a symbol for our intuitive mind and soulfulness appears in the summation of a conversation that took place in 1932 between Carl Jung, the

Swiss psychiatrist, and Ochwiay Biano (which means "Mountain Lake"), the Native American chief of the Taos Pueblo in New Mexico. The gist of this conversation has been reported numerous times, including by Jung himself in his semiautobiographical *Memories, Dreams, Reflections.*

Mountain Lake felt comfortable enough with Jung to offer candid criticism of nonnative Americans: they were never easy, always restless, he said. They were always seeking, never satisfied. When Jung asked why he thought that was the case, Mountain Lake replied, "They say that they think with their heads."

"Why of course," Jung said. "What do you think with?"

"We think here," Chief Mountain Lake told him, and pointed to his heart.[3]

To think with one's heart is to make use of the intuition that arises out of mindfulness and reflection. It's not to be confused with impulsiveness, which feels driven by the heart but in fact results from a lack of balance and connection.

Wholehearted Love with a Broken Heart

Is it possible to love with your whole heart even when it's broken? One person who managed this feat is the actor Paul Linke. For nearly a decade, he'd been married to Francesca "Chex" Draper, a musician and composer. The couple had two young children. Then cancer struck. At thirty-something, Chex was diagnosed with a malignant tumor in her breast and had a mastectomy.

"We were sixties people," was the way Paul described himself and Chex in a conversation with me. They slept on a waterbed, used herbal remedies, and birthed their babies at home.

"Chex was deeply conscious of all of life," he told me. "She wouldn't take an antibiotic or squash a spider." So it followed that she refused her doctors' advice to undergo a postsurgical regimen of chemotherapy and radiation, and turned instead to prayer, greens, and grains as alternative treatments. To complicate matters, Chex became pregnant with the couple's third child. Advised by one doctor to have an abortion, she again refused their counsel. It made no sense to her to kill the life within her when she was trying to save her own. "Chex did not surrender easily," Paul told me.

She underwent as many forms of alternative treatment as she could find, including several trips to the Health Life Clinic in Tijuana to take laetrile, an experimental substance made from the kernels of apricots. She also tried fire walking, psychic healing, and visualization. Paul said, "She had a strong will to survive, albeit on her terms."

Paul was deeply conflicted about his wife's choices. He didn't share her point of view about avoiding Western medical treatment. If it had been his decision, he would have undergone chemotherapy. Even when his fear and frustration were at their most intense, however, he remembered something crucial: the decision wasn't his to make. It belonged to his wife.

After Chex died, Paul captured the couple's experience in a one-man play entitled *Time Flies When You're Alive*.[4] In one scene doctors demand that Paul force Chex to have chemotherapy. He feels paralyzed. On the one hand is his wife's right to live and die as she chooses. On the other are dread and terror, not only that he will lose her but also that he will be complicit in her death.

Finally, Paul erupts at the doctors: "What do you want me to do? Throw her up against the wall and shout, ' "YOU WILL HAVE CHEMO!' "?

"No," he says more quietly. "I can't do that. It's not our relationship."

Whatever we may think of the choices this couple made, the

point is that Paul had the courage to stay open and vulnerable in the face of heartbreak. He withstood his own pain because it mattered more to him to honor the distinct personhood of his dying wife. To love wholeheartedly is to want your partner to follow her values and beliefs, because it's through such commitments that she builds her emotional and spiritual core.

The Second Time Around

When we love wholeheartedly, we may sometimes feel super-connected, reminiscent of how we felt in the first, romantic stage of love. The difference between love in the first and fifth stage, however, is profound. Wholehearted love has a totally different intention and source. It begins with a deep knowledge that I'm enough and can extend myself to you from a grounded place rather than from the often desperate belief that I'm nothing without you and will do whatever it takes to be sure you'll love me. It includes good boundaries, knowing where I end and you begin and being able to say no, as well as yes, to your requests.

Author Brené Brown has brought new light and life to the word *wholehearted* in her books and TED talks on "wholehearted living" and "wholehearted parenting." In *The Gifts of Imperfection*, Brown writes, "Here's what is truly at the heart of wholeheartedness: Worthy now. Not if. Not when. We are worthy of love and belonging *now*. Right this minute. As is."[5]

As a research professor at the University of Houston's College of Social Work, Brown has long studied the factors that make an individual wholehearted. She has connected being wholehearted to having the courage to be imperfect and still feel worthy, to letting yourself be seen in the deepest part of your vulnerability.

Because we're "only human," our very limitations are what

connect us most fundamentally to one another. We become wholehearted "not by finding a perfect person, but by learning to see an imperfect person perfectly," observes psychologist and writer Sam Keen.[6] It's the acceptance of our imperfections by another human being that reassures us that we're still whole and worthy of love. First and foremost, we need to feel worthy within ourselves. In addition, the quality of playfulness, the ability to seize the moment, and humor play a vital role in the health of a relationship.

The Bridge to Self-Worth

My client Steve, whom we met in the last chapter, was eventually able to build a solid sense of self-worth — no small feat, given the uniformly dark version of his history that he'd long subscribed to and the shame that accompanied it. For most of his life he had believed that he was unworthy of love and respect. He was undemonstrative and uncommunicative because he didn't expect anyone to appreciate what he had to offer or to say.

Through long, hard work, Steve uncovered and then made sense of new information, which gave him a fuller picture of his family history, with all its complications and contradictions. None of this expansion and alteration would've been possible, however, without his willingness to open up to possibility.

Because he was game, Steve could bridge the gap between the dark and the light, the past and the present. He reconciled the disparate parts of his life to form a whole and, in the process, gained a new, transformative strength. The photographs helped him remember happier times and the magical boy who could relate to all creatures, especially the birds, in the world around him. He was able to see a whole picture, which included both the heartache and the gifts of childhood.

As Steve's picture of his past expanded, so did his image and understanding of himself. No longer did he see himself solely through the eyes of the child who had assumed there must've been something wrong with him to merit such harsh and neglectful treatment. Gradually, he gained enough perspective to take some pride in his survival tactics and accomplishments: his embrace of nature and the companionship of animals, and later his decision to become a scientist.

Once he lightened up on himself, Steve was able to lighten up on others. For the first time he could pity his parents for the suffering they had endured and admire them for their ability to survive. Now he could discern the nuances that are part of every person's history. At last, he could see his imperfect parents perfectly.

Eventually, he found it possible to forgive them, and then to forgive himself. He understood that the supposed safety he created by hardening his heart had been a big mistake. "It really did the opposite," he told me. "It guaranteed that my alienation and loneliness would continue."

As Steve moved away from his old story, he began to remember the happier times that had been hidden from conscious view. He recalled Sundays with his grandparents, holidays at the beach, and learning woodworking with his father. He also saw how he'd carried into his marriage and family life certain positive habits, values, and virtues that he'd learned as a child, including resourcefulness, self-reliance, and patience. These were qualities that his wife, Stephanie, appreciated in him also and ones the couple wanted to pass on to their children.

All these developments pleased Stephanie, who had worried enough about the impact of Steve's silence and remoteness on their children to consider a separation. These types of concerns have been explored by a number of social researchers, who have concluded that children benefit greatly from knowing their family's history. The studies show that children who have the fullest picture of their families benefit the most. That is, those who are filled in on their ancestors' ups and downs, triumphs and failures, appear to have the strongest sense of control over their lives and the highest self-esteem. As Bruce Feiler reports in his book *The Secrets of Happy Families*, children with the most self-confidence have what researchers call a strong "intergenerational self." They know that they belong to something larger than themselves.[7]

At long last Steve had a fuller, richer sense of his family history, of both its tragedy and its capacity to endure and survive. He also had the immense satisfaction of relaying this history to his two young daughters. According to the latest research, this act alone may increase the odds that his family will blossom in new and myriad ways.

The Bridge to Generosity

In this last stage, the love we aspire to comes from a whole heart, not from the dopamine high of infatuation or from those sweet moments when our partner pleases us. More than a feeling, real love shows itself in action. We make generous, often counter-instinctual moves, discussed in chapter 3, which goes against our grain. We set aside the comfort of old habits and the pull of our first instinct to freeze, flee, or fight. We learn to love with our hands open, not closed. As writer Tara Parker-Pope says, "From tribesmen to billionaire philanthropists, the social value of generosity is already well known. But new research suggests it also matters much more intimately than we imagined, even down to our most personal relationships."[8]

Surprisingly, perhaps, we don't have to wait until we actually feel love and affection to rekindle the spark between us. We can get a jump start by making a generous gesture. We can name some quality or attribute in our partner that we appreciate, and tell her so. Sometimes if we simply name what we love, and give thanks for it, we'll generate the same effect, or one that's almost as positive, as if we actually felt the emotion.

Making a morning cup of tea or coffee for our partner, showing appreciation for ordinary things, and saving an article about something he cares about are all examples of the superglue of generosity that holds relationships together.

When I'm wholehearted, I begin to care for others besides my mate. It may start with my family and friends. And then my concern will extend out toward people whom I've never met, and never will, whose stories and plights touch me. My heart is open to "all sentient beings," as Buddhists say — refugees of war, victims of famine, the humpback whale stranded on a public beach. I respond to them through compassion, prayer, or practical action, because this is what it means to live a wholehearted life. And the grace and tenderness that fill me as my heart radiates out in the world are gifts I take home to share with my partner.

The Bridge to Playfulness

Play is often suggested as a way for couples to restore and rebuild their bridges. The suggestion is fine, as far it goes. Almost every animal species engages in some form of play. They splash or tumble or roll over one another. They scamper or squeal or squawk with delight. Researchers say that play serves a purpose — it teaches skills, including how to cooperate, and it relieves stress.

But engaging in play has its problematic side, too. Organized games and sports aside, play is a spontaneous, intuitive pursuit. Kids play naturally, but many of us lose the ability as we age. To be told to "go and play," however, is as about as useful as to be told to "go and create." Generally speaking, play isn't a straightforward process. And then there is the question of time, and the fundamental priorities of modern life that may leave little room for fun. "We love the idea of having more play in our marriage, but how do we fit play into our busy day?" ask Elaine Braff and Robert Schwarz in *We're No Fun Anymore*, their book about the power of play in cultivating joyful marriages.[9]

We can give ourselves the opportunity for play to occur and then see what happens. Just as we practice being generous even when we don't feel like it, we make time for play even when it's not our first instinct and we have many "more important" things to do. Earlier in this book we read about the two scientists Fred and Marge, the couple who took a vacation to Costa Rica, where they watched giant leatherback turtles emerge from the sea and lay their eggs on the beach in the moonlight. The sighting of the turtles rekindled their interest in each other as a couple. The fact that Fred and Marge shared a keen scientific interest and a warm and affectionate feeling for these remarkable creatures had much to do with their renewed interest in each other. They came away eager to work together to save the turtles. Still, the unexpected renewal of their bond occurred because they cleared space on their calendars for something unscheduled to happen.

To consciously allot ourselves the space and time for spontaneity is important, because one of the most common barriers to wholeheartedness arises out of the decisions we make about how to manage our time.

In the first stage of love, time is plentiful. Somehow we carve out huge numbers of hours from our overbooked appointment calendars and allocate them to being together. Recently I talked with Doug, a hardworking engineer and single parent of three kids who had fallen in love with Lexi, a half-time mom with a time-and-a-half job. I wondered how these two ever got together, given the challenges of their demanding jobs and the needs of their young children.

"I don't really know how we do it," Doug told me with a laugh. "The kids keep us hopping, and we do have to produce for our companies, but we find time for each other all the same. One of us will drop by the other's house, and then suddenly we've spent an hour making love, laughing, telling stories from our lives. Then it's back to work. Still, it's amazing how much time we can find, just because we want to."

Ask yourself when you and your partner last played with a whole heart. What excuses do you have — and I'm sure they're all legitimate — not to spend more time together? Imagine that yours is a new relationship, like Doug and Lexi's, and that you're madly in love and at the height of the first stage. What would you do to get unstructured time together, time that might allow something unexpected to emerge?

Flirting and lovemaking often come naturally at the beginning of a relationship and are vital ways for couples to play. These sweet pleasures certainly can continue if we remain open to possibility and opportunity. Consider doing something entirely new together: inviting friends you don't know well to dinner, taking a hike, buying tickets to see Chinese acrobats or a local garden show. To pursue novelty in our lives together can be a lighter, more indirect alternative, without any of the pressure we might otherwise feel to go out there and have fun on command. The old adage "Variety is the spice of life" is a truism because it's, well, true. Studies show that that novelty adds satisfaction to relationships. So take turns inviting each other to do something fresh and untried. You may find it unexpectedly invigorating — and just plain fun.

The Bridge to Seizing the Moment

Author Gail Sheehy writes movingly about the long struggle that she and her late husband, the magazine editor and journalist Clay Felker, endured as he battled throat cancer over the course of seventeen years. Slowly but surely, the tenacious cancer took away everything he loved, until finally he was unable even to read.

As she watched the man she loved slowly and cruelly succumb to the disease, Gail endured both emotional and physical trauma. Yet, right up to the end, she remained wholehearted in her search for new ways that she and Clay could experience playfulness and joy. In an excerpt from *Passages in Caregiving*, Gail describes one of the last evenings she and Clay managed to enjoy themselves:

> Then I said, "Do you want to do one great thing, darling? Something wonderful?"
>
> He nodded vigorously.
>
> "How about we go out and hear some jazz?"
>
> "Tonight?"
>
> "Tonight."
>
> He shook his head up and down.
>
> I ran to the computer and Googled [a nearby club]. "The show starts in two hours — think we can we make it?"...
>
> He wheeled himself to his closet and picked out a linen jacket, a deep blue shirt, and a suede cap. He allowed me to touch up his face with tinted sunscreen and wheel him in front of the full-length mirror.
>
> "How's that for handsome?" I asked. He looked pleasantly surprised to see a picture of normalcy.
>
> [At the club,] a giant window wall opened to a sweeping view across Central Park....A nearly full moon was rising over the city of fables, his beloved city....When the drums kick-started an up-tempo piece, Clay's fingers drummed on the table. He was a drummer as a boy. For the next hour and a half, Clay sat tall and straight in his wheelchair and drank in the music as his sustenance.
>
> We were back in our apartment shortly before midnight. But Clay was not the least bit tired. He wanted to talk.

He gripped my hands and said clearly: "That was a magical evening."[10]

Clay died two days later.

Gail's story is full of tenderness and a sense of daring and adventure, despite the undercurrent of pain. Her anecdote is a sterling example of how wholehearted living can make our hearts whole.

To go to a jazz club wasn't novel for Clay, I might add. As a boy, he'd sought out the music of Duke Ellington and Ella Fitzgerald. It was Gail's spontaneous suggestion that they go that particular night that was an inspired mix of playfulness, spontaneity, and a deep honoring of her husband's life.

Of our five senses, sound is the one with the most staying power. To go to a club was an impromptu return trip to Clay's earlier roots in the delights of music. Gail's invitation reconnected her husband with one of the touchstones of his life. Even after seventeen years together, with most of those shadowed by his illness, Gail thought about what would feed her husband's heart and soul. Even when she was utterly exhausted in body, mind, and heart, she led her partner out on the town for one last jaunt into the music that had so nourished his life.

The Bridge to Laughter

Humor certainly breaks down barriers: it relieves tension, helps people feel closer, and boosts energy. It's also a way to build a bridge. Sometimes even the edginess of black humor can deepen a bond.

Who would think that life with a dying spouse could provoke laughs? Paul Linke confirmed this unlikely phenomenon in an interview with the *Los Angeles Times* about his last two years with his wife, Chex, before her death from cancer in 1986.[11]

These years weren't as unremittingly dark as one might imagine, he said. The couple had always laughed at things, made jokes, remembered stories from their lives, chuckling over their human foibles. The knack never left them.

"I must stress the humor," he says in another article in *People* magazine in 1989. "We laughed the whole way. I remember holding each other, both of us crying, and then we'd start laughing because it was so intense — just laughing at how much we were crying."[12]

But when Chex died, Paul was overcome by shock and sorrow. Numb, terrified, and alone with three children to care for, he described himself as a man with a broken heart.

Eventually, Paul found a way to channel his grief. With the encouragement of friends, he expanded the eulogy he gave at Chex's funeral into a play (as mentioned on page 171). He presented it as a one-man show in Santa Monica's Powerhouse Theater in 1987 to critical acclaim. Later the play was picked up by HBO and turned into a television drama. Paul subsequently reshaped the play into book form, which he subtitled "A Real-Life Love Story."

Paul healed through creative work that reached the hearts of everyone lucky enough to be moved to tears and laughter by it. Paul's writing had much the same effect as the one described in the first line of Psalm 30:11: "You turned my wailing into dancing." The way he expressed his grief is also reflected in an observation by Jewish mystical rabbi the Baal Shem Tov, who was quoted as saying, "There are three ways to mourn — to weep, to be silent, and to sing."[13]

Logan, one of our beloved Jack Russell terriers, died recently. Both my husband and I were very sad as we recalled the fourteen years of delight he brought us. One morning when I felt especially mournful, my husband reminded me of the strange and funny way Logan used to yawn. We tried to describe this unique yawn, which ended with a very loud squeak. Then Tim tried to imitate it, and we nearly doubled over laughing. After that, we really got going and took turns trying to nail a "Logan yawn." We never quite captured the sound, but we smiled and joked that morning before finally taking our showers, putting on our grown-up clothes, and going out into the world.

Later in the day, I sat in on a long meeting with some associates to discuss financial planning. Suddenly the morning's antics leaped to mind. As I sat listening to deeply serious people talk about annuities and yields and technology trends, I tried not to laugh out loud at the memory of our dog-yawn imitations. Inside, I felt lit up by warmth and a secret grin.

A Spirited Challenge

Play, novelty, and laughter are three fine ways to build bridges. It diminishes them in no way to point out, however, that wholeheartedness requires of us something beyond tactics and skills. As a quote attributed to Erich Fromm put it, "Love isn't something natural. Rather it requires discipline, concentration, patience, faith, and the overcoming of narcissism. It isn't a feeling, it is a practice."[14]

We need to accept that love is more than a feeling: our attitudes and behavior constitute its outer form. As Fromm so wisely observed, our love is burnished through practice — the steady application of discipline, concentration, patience, and faith.

As we climb the mountain of wholeheartedness, we need to seek out teachers and role models to teach and inspire us along the way. The world's great spiritual leaders, as well as our heroic and legendary figures, serve to remind and reassure us that others before us learned how to love well and that there is a light to show us the way. A bumper sticker asks, "What would Jesus do?" Why not use it as a model to pose your own question about your teacher of choice? "What would Buddha (or Saint Francis of Assisi or Einstein or fill in your own mentor) do?"

Ask that question, especially when your instinct tells you to freeze, flee, or fight. A wise teacher can inspire us as we take up the challenges of living intimately with someone and help us to grow into the kind of loving and mature adult we'd like to be.

For centuries spiritual paths have been conceived of as solo journeys: mystics go to the desert, sadhus wander around with a begging bowl, and monks and nuns retire to monasteries or hermitages. Yet a solitary route to spirituality isn't the only way — or even necessarily the preferable one. "It's easy to be a holy man on the top of a mountain," says actor Bill Murray, playing a character in the film *The Razor's Edge*, based on a novel written in 1944 by W. Somerset Maugham. In the story, a World War I veteran seeks peace from his combat trauma, high in the Asian mountains. He resists a return to the "real world" because he fears he'll lose the tranquil sense of well-being he found in the peaks of India.

This theme is found throughout literature — the conflict between our desire to escape the world of other human beings and our desire to dwell within it. Couples the world over experience this conflict. It's easy to be compassionate and generous when you don't have to compromise. It's relatively simple to live peacefully when you're not regularly challenged by a person who sometimes inconveniences you with her decisions, embarrasses you with her choices, and drives you crazy with her "otherness." It's interesting to notice how many of the people we identify as the greatest spiritual teachers are single (and childless as well)!

All major religious traditions carry basically the same message: that love, compassion, and forgiveness should be part of our ongoing relationships.[15]

The same message is found in indigenous healing traditions and in mythological stories, whose teachings reliably point to the practices of gratitude, compassion, and forgiveness. What matters most, says the Dalai Lama, is that we live these virtues in our daily lives. Here it is the action that counts. It's through practice that we overcome the narcissism that Fromm spoke of above. Our relationship is one place to develop this practice, and our partner is one person with whom we have the opportunity to learn.

From this perspective, a couple can envision their life together as a journey toward personal and spiritual development. They can view their unique challenges as the chance to integrate universal qualities of spirit, such as patience, mercy, and kindness. A wholehearted relationship offers us regular opportunities to grow, inside and out. We begin inside ourselves as we counter our instinctual or habitual reactions, temper our negative judgments, and soothe the tensions that can create barriers. We continue outside ourselves as we reach out to accommodate and make room for another, who is both our partner and a distinct individual in his or her own right. As we grow in kindness, generosity, and tolerance, we will be able to fall back on these resources, especially in times of stress and disappointment.

Vive la Différence

We've seen how a couple can move through the last stage of love successfully. After much struggle, Charlie and Megan recommitted to their marriage and pledged to build a new relationship based on the best of what they had discovered in the two years following "the mess," which was how they referred to their marital breakdown. Does this mean that they rode off into the sunset on white horses, hand in hand, smiling, laughing, cherishing, and touching ("wholeheartedly") until the day they died? Of course not.

Writer and psychoanalyst Ethel Person describes it this way:

> Look, in any good relationship there have to be bursts of anger and disagreement. And in those moments, if some-

body asked, "Are you in love?" you'd say, "Are you kidding me?" But those become part and parcel of the journey. We have the capacity to repair relationships — it's like having a scratch that heals. In other words, our psychological makeup has built-in healing mechanisms the same way our body does. You have to have enough conviction in the strength of the bond that you can risk some disagreement. You have to be able to take a hit.[16]

From time to time Charlie still found himself shocked anew by the image of Megan with another man. He relived the force of the betrayal with all the outrage he'd felt when he first found out. Often he wondered why he ever moved so far from the farmland he loved. Although he found great satisfaction in raising chickens and growing vegetables in his suburban garden, he nonetheless sometimes longed for the incomparable aroma of sage, pine, and freshly plowed field.

From time to time, he questioned what he was he doing with a woman like Megan. Sure, she had made some big changes. Life definitely was a lot more interesting since she'd gotten into aikido and bought a horse, but Megan was still Megan. She still subscribed to season tickets to the symphony (which he continued to find boring), and she still persisted in correcting his storytelling if it was the least bit exaggerated (as if exaggeration wasn't what made a story great, Charlie argued on his own behalf).

Megan, too, had her moments of ambivalence. At times thoughts of James would flicker through her mind. She'd feel a pang at the memory of how cultured and sophisticated he was. She missed him. What would it have been like to live with him, she wondered, instead of a man who couldn't understand how disgusting it was to lie on top of a Thai silk bedspread in his running shoes? That particular example of Charlie's slovenly ways could still make her fume.

Yes, sometimes the two of them felt their differences made them an impossible fit. The difference was that they no longer let these contrasts define them as a couple. As they each became more wholehearted in themselves, their relationship became spacious enough to allow more tolerance, humor, and acceptance of each other. They found themselves far less likely to ask the other, "Why aren't you me?" Now they even found it possible to laugh at their differences — at least most of the time. They were more apt to notice what worked between them than what didn't.

Over time, each partner became kinder, more tolerant, and more understanding of the other. These changes gave rise to a new inner experience of well-being, which in turn encouraged them to find new ways to better fit together and move forward as playmates, partners, and deep friends who had weathered some mighty storms together.

Megan and Charlie also simply appreciated each other more. Because they had come so close to losing their marriage, they remained aware of the fundamental fragility of any relationship. They understood how easy it was to destroy a connection and how much time, effort, and energy went into repair and reconstruction. They had no intention of taking for granted all they had rebuilt together.

Sometimes the romantic feelings of stage one reemerged, infusing them with joy and desire. Other times they fell back into Disillusionment and, occasionally, even despaired about the infinity loops that still had the power to trap them. But their periods of misery became much briefer, and they found that they could rebalance themselves more quickly. Mostly they were grateful for a relationship that had withstood serious challenges and kept delivering new and better ways to nourish them, both as individuals and as a couple.

Wholeness as We Change

As I write this chapter, I've just learned that close friends have decided to move to another state, a colleague has died unexpectedly, and our longtime family doctor has decided to change careers. Although I understand that we can't stop the train of life, and although I teach other people about the value of acceptance, I greeted each piece of news with resistance and sadness.

Not all changes are imposed on us. Some changes we choose freely — to travel to another country, say, or to renovate a house. Some changes fulfill our dreams: we land a terrific job, or our child gets into the college of her choice. Even so, nearly every change is bittersweet, if only because it unsettles us.

In a long-term relationship, many changes occur as we travel through love's stages. Each time a shift occurs, so does an opportunity to practice wholehearted love rather letting our fears rule us. Sometimes, of course, we take hold of such an opportunity only after we've passed through a painful dynamic within the relationship.

"George and I thought we had everything worked out," said Millie, an attractive woman in her midseventies. She was speaking to seven other couples who were attending the Love Cycles program. "We had settled the score on all kinds of things during our forty years together. We agreed to disagree on many things, and most often we even felt a reemergence of our early romance."

Millie continued: "But then a new issue came up: Who had the better memory? We started to argue about which one of us was right about a dentist appointment, or what a friend had said at dinner, or what we had agreed to do on our vacation. The arguments grew meanspirited because of our determination to prove the other wrong. One day I suddenly realized that our arguments weren't about the facts at all. They were all about fear

—— fear that our minds were falling apart. I realized that George might be absolutely right: something very scary might be happening to my mind." Although she was speaking about a serious issue, Millie's lighthearted touch allowed the audience to laugh gently with understanding.

Then someone asked, "So what does it mean to be whole, when everything about being a human being is so impermanent?"

Millie answered, "I don't pretend to have a clue. But I can tell you what we did. We'd spent so much time over the years trying to live together with care and understanding, that when I said to George that I thought what was under our squabbles was fear of getting old, he nodded and said, 'Well, we can still hug each other.'

"At that point, the only thing left to do was to just shut up and hold one another for a while. We felt for each other, all right. We were the exact same age, and we had the exact same problem. We might be falling apart, but we're falling together."

The hug shared by Millie and George was a sign of their solidarity, but the challenge to be whole in the midst of change and impermanence remains. Each season of a long life together brings changes. Children are born, parents grow old, dreams come true and then dissolve. Each incident brings with it its own kind of stress, along with our old instincts to freeze, flee, or fight, or to blame the other, bicker, or paper over our differences. No matter how well we've worked things out with our partner in one season, they can fall apart in the next. We find our way together and lose it again with each new change. It's all very human.

The Gift of a Glimpse

We never arrive at wholeheartedness and expect to stay there; we just get to spend more time there if we practice love along the way. When we find ourselves in old loops and shut-down places, we can remember more quickly how to move out of them and let go of hurts and annoyances, the way Millie and George did. Remember, this kind of love is a practice, and our relationship is the grist for the mill. This remains true even when we find ourselves racing at full tilt around the loop of love cycles, sometimes sprinting through all five in just a few hours!

To be wholehearted, then, is to know we won't arrive; we won't cross a bridge and finally "get there." Paradoxically, that's what creates wholeness — our acceptance that perfection is beyond our reach. The gift we gain through the daily practice of love is to be more wholly present in each moment and to open ourselves to all of life with a full heart. The love that blossoms is real.

Remember how expansive your heart was in the beginning, when your partner showered you with abundant appreciation for all the wonders you bestowed? Back then it was so easy to notice all that your lover did right and to let go of the small stuff. As we entered the first stage of love, we experienced the glittering possibilities of the relationship. Now, in the last stage, our recollection of that potential may help us to find our way back to the good things we had.

As we know, this time we must do without the magic potion of early infatuation. To recapture the early promise of love, we need to take the path to our own best selves — distinct and independent, open and caring. This is the journey of a lifetime, and the very essence of wholehearted loving.

Chapter Twelve

LOVE IS
AN INSIDE JOB

We do not see the world as it is,
we see the world as we are.

— attributed to the Talmud and to ANAÏS NIN

As a counselor to couples for many years, I've learned to spot the distinctive stages we travel through over the course of an intimate relationship. I wrote this book to share what I've learned about the Merge, Doubt and Denial, Disillusionment, Decision, and, finally, Wholehearted Loving.

Although these stages are predictable, even inevitable, we have the power to choose how to travel through them as self-aware actors who are in charge of our lives. The purpose of this book has been to show you how — with courage, persistence, and compassion. This last chapter summarizes some of the ideas that have been presented throughout the book, with the hope of conveying the gist of its most important messages before you go. Let's start with a review of the five stages.

Cycles and Choices

The first stage, the Merge, fueled by a delicious and powerful love potion, may lead us to fall in love with an inappropriate partner. Despite the power of the potion, we choose what to do with our feelings. Do we fan the flames of a fire, which signals danger, or do we control our passion and turn our attention elsewhere?

If we choose to move with our partner into stage two, Doubt and Denial, we wake up from our trance of infatuation and begin to wonder whether this relationship is really the best choice for us. What now? We can choose to look carefully at our partner and assess his ability to collaborate, manage conflict and disappointment, and accept responsibility for his choices and troubles. Can we feel strongly attracted to someone and yet admit to ourselves that this person is not a good choice for us? If so, are we able to say no to the relationship?

During this second stage, the spotlight shines on the flaws of our beloved. If we decide to remain in the relationship, typically we now invest a lot of energy in getting our lover to become our ideal partner. At the same time, we also catch glimpses of our own least-likeable parts, for example, how we react when our partner doesn't agree with us (press our point harder) or complains about something we have or haven't done (perhaps we counterattack with a complaint of our own.) Each of us is forced to give up our dream of perfect, unconditional love in which our partner always sees the best in us and says the right thing, never embarrasses us, and reads our mind so that he can please us in every way possible.

As our disappointment escalates, so do our biological responses to stress: we prepare for war, we retreat, or we don camouflage. Welcome to the third stage: Disillusionment. As differences continue to emerge, your proclivities to defend and preserve yourself may grow even stronger: you may believe that you're always in the right and that everything should be done your way.

Alternatively, perhaps you're the kind of person who cannot bear conflict. You shut your ears to every dissonant chord and pretend everything is wonderful — or at least tolerable.

The point is, you have chosen how to respond. You will continue to make choices as you move through love's stages. As Disillusionment sets in, we can try our best to offer goodwill and kindness, even as tension thickens. As the "Why aren't you me?" argument gathers momentum, we can decide to loosen up a bit and allow more than one truth to be present in the relationship.

In this third stage, when our brain signals major alarm, it is particularly vital to choose to move from reactivity to rationality. When we are calmly present, we are free to act for the highest good of the relationship rather than out of fear and neediness.

Of course, because we're thoroughly human, we won't always respond to our lover from our highest self. At times, jealousy, anger, hurt, and pride will get the best of us. Then what? Can we apologize, make amends, and take responsibility for how we behaved, despite what our partner did to upset or annoy us? We have the power to make that choice.

Let's say that when we reach the fourth stage — Decision— we make the choice to part ways. Can we wish our former partner the best? If that's too hard, can we at least not wish him or her the worst?

If our partner decides to leave us, the situation presents a particularly rich opportunity to grow. The child in us may wail, "There are only two reasons a person would leave me: Either I'm bad, or he is!" Or we can choose to listen to the adult inside us who knows that one person can leave another without either one being bad. It is a life choice that may hurt us, but it will not destroy us.

Alternatively, if we decide to remain together, we have the opportunity to learn the lessons that will help to make us the best person we can be, while also giving our relationship the chance to grow and deepen.

Practicing the Six Cs

How do we begin to love this way — from the inside out? I suggest that you start by practicing the "Six Cs," which are choice, commitment, celebration, compassion, cocreation, and courage. If you and your partner commit to developing these qualities and behaviors, you will succeed in the fifth and final stage of love — Wholehearted Loving. Let's take a closer look at these Six Cs to get a sense of the purpose and power of each one.

Choice. A chief component of a healthy relationship is recognizing that our every act — physical, financial, sexual, spiritual, and emotional — involves a choice, even when we imagine ourselves to be helpless. There's an irony here: only when we feel capable of living well on our own can we choose intimate partnership freely and fully. To be able to say yes to a relationship with a whole heart, we need to know we can also say no and thrive on our own. We're the leaders of our own lives.

Commitment. When we are committed to someone, our participation in the relationship is unqualified. We mean to stick around for the entire ride, not just to enjoy the side trip of romantic love before jumping off. We promise ourselves and our partner that we will work hard to enrich and deepen the relationship, which includes taking the time to make it a priority. Commitment also involves an honest examination of the fears and other limitations in ourselves that make love and collaboration with our partner challenging. Commitment includes a pledge to ourselves that we will do the inside work necessary to make the relationship flourish.

Celebration. First and foremost, let your partner know that he or she is fantastic! Learn to pay attention to what works between the two of you; discover small rituals of connection; and find times and ways to play, enjoy each other, and make love that you can integrate into your everyday lives. At the same time, understand that your primary job is to find your own unique purpose and fulfill it. All spiritual traditions emphasize that each person has his or her own calling, and that to discover and celebrate it is our life's work. Self-actualization and connection can be nurtured at the same time — one doesn't exclude the other.

Compassion. Each of us struggles with the human condition, and we must extend compassion to ourselves and to our partner. Note: Compassion is not the same as indulgence. We can maintain clear boundaries and honor our needs for safety and accountability, even while understanding each other's struggles and vulnerabilities. We can stretch to see conflicts from the other's perspective rather than remaining mired in our own point of view. We can make the effort to cultivate interest in each other rather than passing judgment, and to respond with openheartedness even when our instinct is to close up like a clam. We can forgive ourselves and forgive our partner, again and again. Our stumbles are as much a part of the journey as our successes.

Cocreation. One of the most powerful skills a couple can develop is the shared creation of effective ways to manage conflict, communicate, share decisions, and support each other in difficult times. Cocreation can also involve the pursuit of common interests that extend the relationship beyond its customary "you-me" borders. It's healthy for couples to broaden their lives together, be it through family or community connections, creative projects, intellectual pursuits, sports, music, travel, spiritual practice, friendships, or other endeavors that you both find rewarding. We cocreate when we discover satisfying activities to do together rather than just being together. These joint endeavors can create larger meaning in our relationship.

Courage. Bravery is a prerequisite to moving forward as a couple. We need the courage to confront ourselves and our partners with awareness, honesty, and love. Courage means squarely facing our fears and limitations. It involves challenging our expectations and assumptions about who our partners are, about who they should and shouldn't be. It means making changes when they are called for. It is feeling compassion for the whole of our human condition — mine, yours, that of our families, and even of people we feel have wronged us. Bravery is finding a way to laugh at ourselves, too.

From the Inside Out

The people who come into our lives enrich and challenge us. Through these relationships, we're able to see ourselves more clearly. The health of our connections with one another depends a great deal on what goes on inside us — our inner resources, our lingering demons, and our motivation to grow and change.

Some of us are lucky enough to have the same partner for a long stretch. But as good as a relationship can be, our emotional and spiritual life journey begins and ends within us. In this sense, every relationship is an inside job. Inside us is where it starts — and where it finishes, too.

Joseph Campbell, the great American mythologist and writer, believed that the world's most important myths and legends share a similar theme.[1] The journey for each of us, as a hero or a heroine, is to search for the "magic elixir" — our true nature. We may think of this as our higher self, our spiritual nature, or our mature self.

The hero's journey is a powerful metaphor for the couple's path. Two people walk the road together for a time, giving each other the strength and courage to discover that magic elixir within. This is not a quick or easy undertaking. It is best taken on by the courageous and practiced by the patient and has been most elegantly described by the poet Rainer Maria Rilke: "For one human being to love another human being; that is perhaps the most difficult task that has been given to us, the ultimate, the final problem and proof, the work for which all other work is mere preparation."[2]

"That Love is all there is, / is all we know of Love," wrote poet Emily Dickinson, joining sages, singers, writers, and holy teachers who espouse the marvel, agony, and transformational power of this tiny word.[3] This mysterious force turns warriors into cowards and cowards into heroes. It is responsible for heinous crimes, outrageous acts, stunning poetry, and world wonders. The Taj Mahal, the "crown jewel" of India, constructed as an act of love, reminds us of the advice of the spiritual masters: learning to love provides a key to enlightenment and transcendence. Love has the power to help us heal old traumas and bear unimaginable burdens.

It can open us to the deepest wellspring of what it means to be a human being, taking us into the mystery of oneness, of joining and letting go, of accepting the frailty of our humanness while celebrating its magnificence. Our faith in love brings us back again and again to love's journey, the journey to wholeheartedness — the journey home.

WHAT LOVE STAGE ARE YOU IN?
A Quick Quiz by Pepper Schwartz and Linda Carroll

Though at times all the stages in this book might reso-
nate with you, you will be primarily in one stage at a time. How
to get a grasp on it? Here is a simple quiz that will help you assess
what stage you are in. Knowing this will help you know how to
deal with it most appropriately. On a scale from 1 to 10, rate how
true each of these statements is for you. At the end of the questions we will tell you how to score yourself and how to interpret
your score.

The Merge

____ This relationship makes me feel wonderful; I'm "walking
on air."

____ I am amazed at how beautifully our interests, beliefs, and experiences seem to dovetail.

____ We can talk for hours, staying engaged and fascinated.

____ I feel that we are linked in a very special way, possibly on a spiritual level.

____ We sleep close together, often keeping our arms around each other.

____ Though we've been together a relatively short time, I think I may have found the perfect person for me.

____ The kinds of things that have annoyed me about other partners seem to roll off my back this time around.

____ When we are apart, I long to be with him/her.

____ Our lovemaking seems effortless and complete, almost magical.

____ When I'm with my partner, ordinary things — like going to the grocery store or walking the dog — are almost ridiculously fun.

Doubt and Denial

____ Some of the traits that I once found alluring, amusing, or exciting in my partner are beginning to irritate me.

____ I find that I am more critical of my partner, and I notice that he/she has begun to criticize me.

____ We sleep farther away in bed than we used to, except when we make love.

____ Our sexual connection doesn't feel magical anymore (although I often pretend it does).

____ I am beginning to see many worrisome flaws in my partner and wondering how I missed them.

____ I am afraid that I may have failed at love again.

____ We argue too much.

___ I am starting to miss some of the people and activities I used to care about before I got into this relationship.

___ I long for the feelings of ease and effortless connection we used to have.

___ I wonder whether this is going to work out.

Disillusionment

___ I am disappointed that my partner is so different from the person I thought he/she was.

___ We argue about the same things over and over.

___ I find myself getting (secretly) bored, and even annoyed, by the same old stories he/she tells.

___ I no longer feel I can share my real thoughts with my partner.

___ I often stay angry about things my partner has said or done; when we attempt to talk about the trouble, I often feel defensive.

___ We seem sexually incompatible.

___ I wonder how I missed some of the obvious signs of trouble with this person.

___ We can sleep in the same bed and not touch all night long.

___ I fear I have made a commitment to the wrong person.

___ I'm not sure I'm in love anymore.

Decision

___ My partner and I are leading almost parallel lives.

___ I can barely remember why I fell in love.

___ I am exhausted by the struggles in our relationship.

___ The problems we face seem to outweigh the benefits of staying together.

___I have thought about separation, and I fantasize about my life away from this relationship.

___I feel that our relationship is at a crossroads: we have to move in one direction or the other.

___I worry that my health is going to suffer — or already is suffering — because of relationship stress.

___I wonder whether I even like my partner anymore.

___I am happier doing things alone or with friends than with my partner.

___I wonder whether our relationship is beyond repair.

Wholehearted Loving

___I recognize that there are ways I have to change in order to make this relationship a great one.

___I am willing to have difficult conversations with my partner and to listen attentively in a new way.

___I feel relaxed with my partner.

___I understand that there are often big differences in how my partner and I experience and react to situations, and I can tolerate these more easily than I used to.

___I am developing new capacities for humility, compassion, gratitude, and generosity in this relationship.

___I love to sleep with my partner and am also comfortable sleeping on my own.

___In some ways, I feel more in love with my partner than when we first met, but it's also okay not to feel this intensely all the time.

___I feel more whole in my relationship than I ever have.

___Our sexual connection has matured into an easy, comfortable, and fulfilling experience. When sex doesn't work between us, we can laugh and let it go.

___ This relationship is helping me become the best person I can be.

Take a look at which stage has the most 9 and 10. If there is a preponderance of 9s and 10s in one section versus another, chances are that is the stage you are in. If you are evenly split between one stage and an adjacent stage, you may be in transition.

ACKNOWLEDGMENTS

I have had the great fortune of studying with many wonderful teachers and guides. Some of the ideas in this book that I have described, paraphrased, or borrowed from (and re-created in my own words and with my own focus) represent a part of what I have learned from them. Below are the people who have most influenced me in my practice with couples and in my writing of this book:

Dr. Lori Gordon and the PAIRS Foundation

Drs. Hal and Sidra Stone and the Delos Foundation

Dr. Harville Hendrix, Helen L. Hunt, and the Imago Foundation

Dr. Pat Love and the Hot Monogamy Training Program

Dr. Ellyn Bader and Dr. Peter Pearson and the Couples Institute

Sam Keen and his life's work on the Art of Passionate Living

Hedy and Yumi Schleifer and the Relationship Builders Program

Dr. Helen Fisher and her work on understanding love — historically, scientifically, and psychologically.

Pema Chödrön, who helps me remember that nothing stays the same and that the cycle is really a spiral, always moving and changing into something new and often unexpected. Wholehearted Loving is a place to work toward, not a place we land on indefinitely, and Chödrön has helped to deepen my understanding and acceptance of this essential impermanence.

I would like to express my deepest gratitude to:

My agent, Barbara Moulton, who took a risk because she "got it" and believed in *Love Cycles*.

Deborah Szekely and her daughter, Sarah Livia, who founded Rancho La Puerta and nourished it into the paradise it has become, giving me a place to write, learn, and replenish.

Victoria Larrea, for her ongoing encouragement, support, and modeling of steady graciousness in the face of incessant demands.

The guests I have taught at Rancho La Puerta, who in turn have taught and inspired me.

Mary Ann McCready of Nashville and author and dear friend Marilyn Mason, each of whom revitalized this book (and me) in immeasurable ways.

Dr. Pepper Schwartz for her tremendous contribution on sexuality, and her generosity and encouragement.

My deepest thanks also go to:

Marie France, who has been with me for three books and knows how to weave my vast, often seemingly unrelated ideas into a common language and breathe new life into my characters.

Marian Sandmaier, the editorial genius who takes an ordinary paragraph and turns it into prose without losing any of my thoughts and ideas, and who gives me ongoing support, suggestions, and challenge.

For the ideas of the cycle and the model, I am grateful to Joseph Campbell and Rick and Char Torsi. Thanks to Rita Jacobs, writer and professor at Montclair State University, who gave me the idea for the title of the book. To Craig Tinus for his wonderful descriptions of birds and other creatures in chapter 10.

I am also grateful to the many couples who don't identify with the label of *heterosexual* and who have to work extra hard to translate and redefine the language of *he* and *she* into more appropriate pronouns, both in our Love Cycles classes and as readers.

My children gave me vital support in a variety of ways. Jaimee King read each word of this manuscript with care and clarity, giving me invaluable feedback, and Nicole Carroll offered long, enlightening conversations about the nature of love in all the stages. I thank Tobias Menely for the ongoing, vivid conversation about play and birds, which enriched the book immensely, and Daniel Menely for sitting through endless talks about Love Cycles at Rancho La Puerta and giving me strong and clever critiques about the anecdotal stories I used in the book.

I thank Suze Bear, who arrived — as she usually does — at just the right moment to help me in immeasurable ways.

My deepest thanks to the special team and dearest friends at Northwest Seminars, each of whom brings unique gifts to students in our many seminars and retreats.

David Long and Deborah Lyman enrich everything with remarkable generosity, humor, and competence in doing whatever needs to be done, including fixing fax machines, cleaning coffee cups and couches, working overtime with couples who feel stuck and, most of all, sharing their extraordinary personal journey to wholehearted love with hundreds of couples in our classes. Thank you for your extra, unexpected gift of abiding and delightful friendship.

My colleague and dear friend Ann Ladd, who brings our students into even deeper self-knowledge with her magnificent spirit, brilliant skills, and defining work on infinity loops.

Dale Rhodes, who has woven the Enneagram into the fabric of our teachings with soul, humor, and seemingly unlimited knowledge.

Thanks to Christine Barraud, my clever, creative daughter-in-law at Big Catch Creative in Wellington, New Zealand, who designed the logo for this book.

Finally and most important, I extend love and deepest gratitude to my husband, Tim Barraud, who has believed in my vision through four decades of cycling and recycling through the stages of love's journey. He has changed and opened his life in unimaginable ways to join me in bringing this work to hundreds of couples and individuals over the past twenty-five years.

ENDNOTES

Chapter 1. The Merge

1. Margaret Mahler (1897–1985), a Hungarian physician, was known for the separation-individuation theory of child development, also known as "developmental ego psychology." She described stages of development from a merged infant into an individualized adult. Ellyn Bader and Peter Pearson borrowed from this model in their book *In Quest for the Mythical Mate: A Developmental Approach to Diagnosis and Treatment in Couples Therapy* (Florence, KY: Brunner/Mazel, 1998), in which they show how couples go through parallel developmental stages with each other. My studies with Bader and Pearson have been an integral part of forming *Love Cycles*.

2. Dr. Helen Fisher has had a profound influence on my understanding of why, how, and who we love. Although I cite her in specific parts of this book, the full body of her work has influenced my understanding of this first stage of love more than anyone else's work. She has conducted

extensive research and written five books on the evolution and future of human sex, love, marriage, and gender differences in the brain; and has done extensive teaching, including giving TED talks. Dr. Fisher is a senior research fellow at the Kinsey Institute and the chief scientific advisor to Match.com (as well as developing their site, Chemistry.com). The vast body of her work can be found at www.helenfisher.com.

3. "Second Baby for Ingrid," *Sunday Times* (Perth, Western Australia), February 3, 1952, www.trove.nla.gov.au/ndp/del/article/59540323.

4. Majid Sadiqi Hasan Abadi, "A Glance at Love in the Transcendent Philosophy," www.mullasadra.org/new_site/english/Paper%20Bank /Gnosis/Majid%20Sadiqi%20Hasan%20Abadi.htm.

5. A detailed description of each of these signs and symptoms can be found in Dorothy Tennov, *Love and Limerence: The Experience of Being in Love* (New York: Stein and Day, 1979). A summary of the signs of limerence can be found in David Sack, "Limerence and the Biochemical Roots of Love Addiction," *Huffington Post*, June 28, 2012, www .huffingtonpost.com/david-sack-md/limerence_b_1627089.html.

6. Intense, passionate feelings of love can provide amazingly effective pain relief, similar to that offered by painkillers or drugs such as cocaine: Tracie White, "Love Takes Up Where Pain Leaves Off, Brain Study Shows," *Stanford School of Medicine*, October 13, 2010, Med.stanford. edu/ism/2010/october/love.html. See also Helen E. Fisher, Arthur Aron, Debra Mashek, Haifang Li, and Lucy L. Brown, "Defining the Brain Systems of Lust, Romantic Attraction, and Attachment," *Archives of Sexual Behavior* 31, no. 5 (October 2002): 313–19, www.helenfisher .com/downloads/articles/14defining.pdf; and A. de Boer, E. M. van Buel, and G. J. Ter Horst, "Love Is More Than Just a Kiss: A Neuro-biological Perspective on Love and Affection," *Neuroscience* 201 (January 10, 2012): 114–24, www.sciencedirect.com/science/article /pii/S030645221101284X.

7. In *The Chemistry of Love* (Boston: Little, Brown, 1983), Michael R. Liebowitz details the discovery of endorphins and chemistry changes in people in this first stage. A description of PEA can be found in Theresa L. Crenshaw, *The Alchemy of Love and Lust: How Our Sex Hormones Influence Our Relationships* (New York: Simon & Schuster, 1997), 55–62.

8. Grant F. Scott, ed., *Selected Letters of John Keats* (Cambridge: Harvard University Press, 1958), 390.

9. Claus Wedekind, Thomas Seebeck, Florence Bettens, and Alexander J. Paepke, "MHC-Dependent Preferences in Humans," *Proceedings of the Royal Society of London* 260, no. 1359 (June 1995): 245–49.

10. Harville Hendrix is best known for his book *Getting the Love You Want*, a *New York Times* bestseller, and he has written several other bestselling books that help couples untangle themselves from these ongoing patterns. As an Imago-trained therapist, I have learned and absorbed a great deal from my training.

    Hendrix's entire body of work has focused on translating object relations theory into a language that makes the theory accessible to the general public. Karl Abraham was the first person to develop object relations theory; Melanie Klein is best known for bringing it to the greater population. This theory suggests that our adult relationships are determined by our first relationships: those of our family, especially our parents. For example, an overbearing father or an abusive mother turns into an Object in the subconscious, and that Object carries into adulthood in our expectations, interactions, and reactions to people who show elements of the same behavior.

11. "Your Brain in Love," *PositScience*, November 13, 2013, www.posit science.com/brain-resources/brain-facts-myths/brain-in-love.

12. Pema Chödrön, *When Things Fall Apart: Heart Advice for Difficult Times* (Boston: Shambhala, 2000), 10.

Chapter 2. Doubt and Denial

1. Bunny Duhl, "The Interpersonal Vulnerability Contract: A Tool for Turning Alienation into Connection with Couples, Families, and Groups" (talk given at the First International Family Encounter, Mexico City, November 15, 1976). See also Ann Ladd, *Heart of Healing: A Therapist's Journey with Clients* (Pueblo West, CO: Fireside, 2010), 111; and Lori H. Gordon and Jon Frandsen, *Passage to Intimacy* (New York: Fireside, 2001), 238–44. In her second book, *Love Knots: How to Untangle Those Everyday Frustrations and Arguments That Keep You from Being with the One You Love* (Palo Alto, CA: Science and Behavior Books, 1997), Gordon provides humorous, familiar, insightful examples of some of the most common loops.

2. Patricia Love and Jo Robinson, *Hot Monogamy: Essential Steps to More Passionate, Intimate Lovemaking* (CreateSpace Independent Publishing Platform, June 6, 2012). See especially chapter 4, "When I'm Hot and You're Not: Resolving Differences in Desire."

3. Love and Robinson, *Hot Monogamy*, 66–94.

Chapter 3. Six Essential Skills

1. "Hedy and Yumi: Crossing the Bridge Documentary" (Miami Beach, FL: Hedy and Yumi Relationship Builders, 2010), DVD, www.hedy yumi.com/2010/06/hedy-yumi-crossing-the-bridge. From their trainings and film, which describes their philosophy (with many demonstrations), I was able to gain a new appreciation of the difference between just listening and really being able to be in the shoes of another person. "Crossing the bridge" refers to being truly able to experience the world as your partner does.

2. Sharon Ellison, *Taking the War out of Our Words: The Art of Powerful Non-Defensive Communication* (Deadwood, OR: Wyatt-MacKenzie Publishing, 2009) 7–23.

3. Christopher Bergland, "The 'Love Hormone' Drives Human Urge for Social Connection," *Psychology Today*, September 12, 2013, www.psychologytoday.com/blog/the-athletes-way/201309 /the-love-hormone-drives-human-urge-social-connection.

4. Matthew McKay, Jeffrey C. Wood, and Jeffrey Brantley, *The Dialectical Behavior Therapy Skills Workbook: Practical DBT Exercises for Learning Mindfulness, Interpersonal Effectiveness, Emotion Regulation, and Distress Tolerance* (Oakland, CA: New Harbinger Publications, 2007), 9–10 and 24–27.

5. John W. Jacobs, *All You Need Is Love and Other Lies about Marriage: How to Save Your Marriage before It's Too Late* (New York: Harper-Collins, 2004), 80.

6. Jon Kabat-Zinn, *Wherever You Go There You Are: Mindfulness Meditation in Everyday Life* (New York: Hyperion, 14), 4.

Chapter 4. Disillusionment

1. Quoted in James Fadiman and Robert Frager, *Personality and Personal Growth*, 6th ed. (Upper Saddle River, NJ: Prentice Hall, 2005), 56. Fadiman and Frager explain, "Individuation means becoming a single, homogeneous being, and, insofar as 'individuality' embraces our innermost, last, and incomparable uniqueness, it also implies becoming one's own self; we could therefore translate individuation as 'coming to selfhood' or 'self-realization.'"

2. Margaret S. Mahler, Fred Pine, and Anni Bergman, *The Psychological Birth of the Human Infant: Symbiosis and Individuation* (Great Britain: Hutchinson, 1975), 92–95.

3. Ellyn Bader and Peter Pearson, *In Quest of the Mythical Mate: A Developmental Approach to Diagnosis and Treatment in Couples Therapy* (Florence, KY: Brunner/Mazel, 1988), 11, 12.

4. Hal Stone and Sidra Stone, *Embracing Your Inner Critic: Turning Self-Criticism into a Creative Asset* (San Francisco: HarperSanFrancisco, 1993), 3–27.

Chapter 5. Seven Normal Troubles

1. Much has been written about depression and living with a depressed partner. Two of the books I recommend are Terrence Real Scribner, *I Don't Want to Talk about It: Overcoming the Secret Legacy of Male Depression* (New York: Scribner, 1998), and Anne Sheffield, Mike Wallace, and Donald F. Klein, *How You Can Survive When They're Depressed: Living and Coping with Depression Fallout* (New York: Three Rivers Press, 1998).

2. Susan Johnson, *Hold Me Tight: Seven Conversations for a Lifetime of Love* (Boston: Little, Brown, 2008). Brown's premise in this book, which has been on the bestseller list since it first came out, is that the underlying trouble in relationship conflicts is the loss of connection, more important than whatever issue people are in conflict over.

3. The Intentional Dialogue, introduced by Dr. Harville Hendrix, is the best process I know for helping couples stay connected: "4 Steps to Healthy Communication: Intentional Dialogue Exercise," Oprah.com, December 7, 2013, www.parapundit.com/archives/003887.html.iwww.oprah.com/relationships/Intentional-Dialogue-Exercise-The-Steps. I also recommend the following film, which shows how the Intentional Dialogue is done and its outcome with couples: "Hedy and Yumi: Crossing the Bridge Documentary" (Miami Beach, FL: Hedy and Yumi Relationship Builders, 2010), DVD, www.hedyyumi.com/2010/06/hedy-yumi-crossing-the-bridge.

   One more excellent tool for understanding and connection is the Dialogue Wheel, taught by Lori H. Gordon of the PAIRS Foundation. This can be found in many places on the web and in Gordon and Jon Frandsen, *Passage to Intimacy* (New York: Fireside, 2001), 85–86.

4. Harriet Lerner's *Marriage Rules: A Manual for the Married and the Coupled Up* Facebook page, accessed November 15, 2013, www.facebook.com/marriagerules.

Chapter 6. Decision

1. Joseph Campbell, ed., *The Portable Jung* (New York: Penguin, 1976), 17.
2. Jack Kornfield, *A Path with Heart* (New York: Bantam, 1993), 15.
3. Pema Chödrön, "Reaching underneath Our Protective Shell," Awakin.org, November 4, 2013, www.awakin.org/read/view.php?tid=976.
4. Quoted in Cathleen Medwick, "Radical Romance Changes Lives,"

Oprah.com, September 22, 2010, www.oprah.com/relationships /Ethel-Person-MDs-Relationship-and-Love-Advice.

5. Laura Munson, "Those Aren't Fighting Words, Dear," *New York Times*, July 31, 2009, www.nytimes.com/2009/08/02/fashion/02love .html?pagewanted=all&_r=0.

6. Jesse Kornbluth, "Her Husband of 20 Years Said, 'I Want Out. I Don't Love You.' She Said, 'I Don't Buy It.' And Then...," *Huffington Post*, March 26, 2010, www.huffingtonpost.com/jesse-kornbluth/this-is-not -the-story-you_b_515018.html.

7. Ibid.

8. "Hedy and Yumi: Crossing the Bridge Documentary" (Miami Beach, FL: Hedy and Yumi Relationship Builders, 2010), DVD, www.hedy yumi.com/2010/06/hedy-yumi-crossing-the-bridge.

9. See Susan Gadoua, *Contemplating Divorce: A Step-by-Step Guide to Deciding Whether to Stay or Go* (Oakland, CA: New Harbinger, 2008), and Cheryl Jarvis, *The Marriage Sabbatical: The Journey That Brings You Home* (Cambridge, MA: Broadway, 2008).

Chapter 8. Our Sexual Cycles

1. Kara Mayer Robinson, "Ten Surprising Health Benefits of Sex," WebMD, October 24, 2013, www.webmd.com/sex-relationships /guide/sex-and-health.

2. Barry McCarthy, "Marital Sex as It Ought to Be, Abstract," *Journey of Family Psychotherapy* 14, no. 2 (2003), www.tandfonline.com/doi /abs/10.1300/J085v14n02_01#preview.

3. *Annie Hall*, directed by Woody Allen (MGM Studios, 1977).

4. Patricia Love and Jo Robinson, *Hot Monogamy: Essential Steps to More Passionate, Intimate Lovemaking* (New York: Penguin, 1995), 66–94.

5. Esther Perel, *Mating in Captivity: Unlocking Erotic Intelligence* (New York: HarperCollins, 2006), 219.

6. N. L McCoy and J. M. Davidson, "A Longitudinal Study of the Effects of Menopause on Sexuality," PubMed.gov, September 7, 1985, www .ncbi.nlm.nih.gov/pubmed/4079820.

7. S. E Trompeter, R. Bettencourt, and E. Barrett-Connor, "Sexual Activity and Satisfaction in Healthy Community-dwelling Older Women," *American Journal of Medicine* 125, no. 1 (January 2012), 37–43, www .amjmed.com/article/S0002-9343(11)00655-3/abstract.

8. Wendy Maltz, "Staying Hot and Sexy at Midlife," Healthysex.com, 1999, www.healthysex.com/page/staying-hot-and-sexy-in-midlife.

9. Barry McCarthy, PhD, "Female Sexual Desire: A Motivating, Empowering Approach," *Psychology Today* blog, January 7, 2014,

www.psychologytoday.com/blog/whats-your-sexual-style/201401
/female-sexual-desire-motivating-empowering-approach.

10. Edith Wharton, *The Age of Innocence* (New York: D. Appleton and
    Company, 1920), 63.

11. James Joyce, *Ulysses* (New York: Oxford University Press, 1998), 732.

Chapter 9. The Fine Art of Differentiation

1. Mary Oliver, *House of Light* (Boston: Beacon Press, 1990), 63.
2. Angeles Arrien, foreword to *Maps to Ecstasy: A Healing Journey for the Untamed Spirit*, by Gabrielle Roth, revised edition (Novato, CA: New World Library, 1998), xv.
3. Lori H. Gordon and Jon Frandsen, *Passage to Intimacy* (New York: Simon & Schuster, 1993), 142.
4. Esther Perel, "How to Put a Healthy Dose of Space and Mystery into Your Relationship," *Esther's Blog*, December 6, 2013, www.estherperel .com/how-to-put-a-healthy-dose-of-space-and-mystery-into-your -relationship.

Chapter 10. Wholehearted Loving: The Barriers

1. Quoted in Rachel Rettner, "Romantic Love Is an Addiction, Researchers Say," LiveScience, July 6, 2010, www.livescience.com/6695-romantic -love-addiction-researchers.html.
2. Helen Fisher, TED talk, Monterey, CA, February 2006, blog.ted.com /2006/09/06/helen_fisher_on.
3. Arthur Aron, Lucy L. Brown, Helen Fisher, "Romantic Love: An fMRI Study of a Neural Mechanism for Mate Choice," *Journal of Comparative Neurology* 493, no. 1 (October 2005): onlinelibrary.wiley.com /doi/10.1002/cne.20772/abstract.
4. Michael Ondaatje, *The English Patient* (New York: Vintage, 1993), 97.
5. M. Scott Peck, *The Road Less Traveled: A New Psychology of Love, Traditional Values and Spiritual Growth* (New York: Simon & Schuster, 1978), 85.
6. Hiroo Onoda, *No Surrender: My Thirty-Year War* (New York: Kodansha, 1974), 14–15.

Chapter 11. Wholehearted Loving: The Bridges

1. Gail Godwin, *Heart: A Natural History of the Heart-Filled Life* (New York: Harper Perennial, 2001), 20.

2. David Richo, *The Sacred Heart of the World: Restoring Mystical Devotion to Our Spiritual Life* (Mahwah, NJ: Paulist Press, 2007), 11–15.

3. C. G. Jung , *Memories, Dreams, Reflections* (New York: Vintage Books, 1989), 247.

4. The scene described came from the HBO film based on Paul Linke's book, *Time Flies When You're Alive: A Real-Life Love Story* (New York: Birch Lane Press, 1993).

5. Brené Brown, *The Gifts of Imperfection: Let Go of Who You Think You're Supposed to Be and Embrace Who You Are* (Center City, MN: Hazelden, 2010), 24.

6. Sam Keen, *To Love and Be Loved* (New York: Bantam, 1999), 42.

7. Bruce Feiler, *The Secrets of Happy Families: Improve Your Mornings, Rethink Family Dinner, Fight Smarter, Go Out and Play, and Much More* (New York: William Morrow, 2013), 42.

8. Tara Parker-Pope, "The Generous Marriage," *New York Times Magazine*, December 11, 2011, well.blogs.nytimes.com/2011/12/08 /is-generosity-better-than-sex/?_r=o.

9. Robert Schwarz and Elaine Braff, *We're No Fun Anymore: Helping Couples Cultivate Joyful Marriages through the Power of Play* (New York: Routledge, 2011), 83.

10. Gail Sheehy, *Passages in Caregiving: Turning Chaos into Confidence* (New York: William Morrow, 2010), 355–56.

11. Don Shirley, "TV REVIEW: Paul Linke Drama on Birth and Death Moves to HBO," *Los Angeles Times*, July 29, 1989, articles.latimes.com /keyword/paul-linke.

12. Joanne Kaufman and Kristina Johnson, "In *Time Flies When You're Alive*, Actor Paul Linke Turns the Last Years of His Wife's Life into Art," August 21, 1989, www.people.com/people/article/o,,2012 1003,00.html.

13. Quoted in Jack Stern, *The Right Not to Remain Silent: Living Morally in a Complex World* (Lincoln, NE: iUniverse, 2006), 97.

14. Erich Fromm, *The Art of Loving* (New York: Harper Perennial, 2006), 109.

15. Mark Alton Rose, *Especially for Christians: Powerful Thought-Provoking Words from the Past* (Lincoln, NE: iUniverse, 2005), 19.

16. Quoted in Cathleen Medwick, "Radical Romance Changes Lives," Oprah.com, September 22, 2010, www.oprah.com/relationships /Ethel-Person-MDs-Relationship-and-Love-Advice.

Chapter 12. Love Is an Inside Job

1. Joseph Campbell, *The Hero with a Thousand Faces* (Novato, CA: New World Library, 2008), 211.
2. Rainer Maria Rilke, *Letters to a Young Poet* (New York: Penguin, 1986), 68.
3. Emily Dickinson, *The Collected Poems of Emily Dickinson* (New York: Barnes & Noble, 2003), 83–86.

INDEX

ABOUT THE AUTHOR

Linda Carroll, MS, has worked as a couples therapist for more than thirty years. In addition to being a licensed therapist, she is certified in Transpersonal Psychology and Imago Therapy, the highly successful form of couples therapy developed by Dr. Harville Hendrix and Dr. Helen LaKelly Hunt, and is a master teacher in the PAIRS Psychoeducation Process. She has studied many modalities of psychological and spiritual work, including Voice Dialogue, Holotropic Breathwork with Dr. Stan Grof, the Four-Fold Way with Angeles Arrien, the Diamond Heart Work of A. H. Almaas, and training with the Couples Institute of Ellyn Bader and Dr. Peter Pearson. She is also certified in the Hot Monogamy program, which helps couples create (or re-create) the passion that makes relationships thrive.

Linda works with a limited number of couples regularly in a new style of "concierge therapy" in which she travels to their home or office for two to six days a year for private, all-day sessions, offering ongoing Skype and phone sessions in between. She teaches workshops and delivers keynote addresses throughout the United States and is a frequent speaker at Rancho La Puerta in Tecate, Mexico. Linda lives in Corvallis, Oregon, with her veterinarian husband, Tim Barraud, and a Jack Russell terrier.

She has five children and nine grandchildren in the States and three "bonus children" and six "bonus grandchildren" in New Zealand. Her website is www.lindaacarroll.com.